A Manual on Nonviolence and Children

Compiled and Edited by
Stephanie Judson

Committee on Nonviolence and Children
Philadelphia Yearly Meeting
Religious Society Of Friends

New Society Publishers

With contributions from Ellen Deacon, Chuck Esser, Ellen Forsythe, Marta Harrison, Stephanie Judson, Karen Zaur, and others.

Hardcover ISBN: 0-86571-035-X
Paperback ISBN: 0-86571-036-8
Printed in the United States

Inquiries regarding permission to reproduce all or part of this book should be addressed to:
New Society Publishers
4722 Baltimore Avenue
Philadelphia, PA 19143

New Society Publishers is a project of New Society Educational Foundation and a collective of Movement for a New Society. New Society Educational Foundation is a non profit, tax-exempt corporation. Tax deductible contributions can be made to any of their projects. Movement for a New Society is a network of small groups and individuals working for fundamental social change through nonviolent action. To learn more about MNS write: Movement for a New Society, 4722 Baltimore Avenue, Philadelphia, PA 19143. Opinions expressed in this book do not necessarily represent agreed-upon positions of either the New Society Educational Foundation or Movement for a New Society.

Acknowledgement is made to the Waldorf Press Publishers, Garden City, New York for permission to quote from Morey and Gilliam, ed., *Respect for Life* (copyright 1974, The Myrin Institute, Inc., 521 Park Ave., New York, NY 10021).

Preface

The Nonviolence and Children Program began in 1969 when members of the Friends Peace Committee in Philadelphia felt that an important way to build a peaceful world would be to develop a program for young children. A small and dedicated volunteer subcommittee with one staffperson was formed under Friends Peace Committee of Philadelphia Yearly Meeting, the local organization of Friends (Quakers). In 1974 the Nonviolence and Children Collective was formed. The collective shared the responsibility for program work and direction, while the Nonviolence and Children Subcommittee maintained general oversight of the program and was formed into a pilot parent support group.

This manual is an outgrowth of the work of the Nonviolence and Children Program, especially during the years 1973–6. Writing this manual was a cooperative effort. As compiler and editor, Stephanie Judson went over each section, often reworking and rewriting it. With the help of numerous people, she saw the manual through various stages to completion. The manual is based on the program's experiences in schools, with parents, teachers, and intergenerational groups. The theory of Reevaluation Counseling was helpful in the collective's experience and in the development of its own thinking.

There are hundreds of people who have contributed to the work of the program and thus to the manual. They are too numerous to list here, yet we would like to thank them warmly. Some of these people appear on the pages of the manual. When we were able to contact people for permission to use their names, we have printed their first and last names. Fictitious first names without a last name appear when we weren't able to reach the person for permission, and in cases where it was appropriate to fictionalize names.

Presently we have one staffperson and an active committee. We have continued to develop and enlarge on the material in this manual through our work with schools, Friends Meetings, parent support groups and other groups of children and adults. Our theme for the current year, 1983–4, is "Empowerment in an Age of Anxiety."

We define empowerment as the process of becoming hopeful and in charge of one's own life which leads to participation in social change. As significant adults in children's lives, whether we are teachers, parents or concerned friends, it is our task to provide children with hope for the future. In addition we need to find ways for children to take action in their immediate lives to counterbalance the feelings of hopelessness and powerlessness that are intensified by the threat of nuclear war.

We see empowerment as a logical outgrowth of the work described in the manual. In order to feel hopeful about the future, we must first feel good about ourselves (affirmed), learn to empathize with others (share feelings), find a supportive community, build confidence through solving our own problems, and make beauty and joy a part of our lives. These steps are the major sections of this book.

As teachers, parents and group facilitators, we have used the theory and techniques described in the manual in numerous settings. We use them to create an atmosphere in our classrooms, homes and workshops as well as setting aside specific times to play the games or lead the exercises.

Our current staffperson, Lorraine Wilson, is developing new theory on how risk-taking can work toward building self-esteem primarily with outdoor/experiential education activities. Kathy Schultz, committee member and teacher, is collaborating with the program this year to develop materials and strategies that lead to a new way of thinking in the nuclear age. She is working with teachers in their classrooms to address the issues of empowerment, complexity of thinking and community building. Lois Dorn's book, *Peace in the Family,* was published this fall by Pantheon Press, and is based on her work with parent support groups while she was a staffperson for the program.

The Nonviolence and Children Committee was formed fourteen years ago to help children and their caregivers develop nonviolent attitudes and skills. In our present work we are helping teachers and parents become adults that children can look to for nurturance and guidance. We are helping them to make their classrooms and homes safe places where risks can be taken. Our hope is that children will grow up to be informed decision makers who seek nonviolent solutions and consider the consequences of their actions for themselves and others. In these ways we are teaching the peacemakers of the future.

We look back with satisfaction and forward with excitement.

Nonviolence and Children Program
Philadelphia, PA.
October 1983

Foreword

Until recently, teaching of nonviolent conflict resolution skills has been largely relegated to private and pacifist-oriented schools. Gradually, however, many of us in other educational environments have begun to connect the continual use of violence to settle disputes with the growing threat of nuclear conflict. We have started to re-educate ourselves and our children towards new ways of thinking that may help avert a nuclear catastrophe. A MANUAL ON NONVIOLENCE AND CHILDREN is a fine resource for educators and others who want to join in the effort of teaching children the skills necessary to resolve conflict without resorting to violence.

Although many of us previously regarded conflict resolution techniques as primarily useful to adults seeking rational solutions to global problems, we now recognize that these same techniques can make our children active participants in resolving the practical problems which arise in their daily lives at home and at school. When you teach children to respond to disagreement, fighting, and differences of opinion through dialogue, mediation, and active listening it immediately empowers them by broadening their range of available responses. As any teacher who has incorporated these techniques into daily classroom procedure can attest, students become better able to respond to every day conflicts with an enhanced sense of choice, fairness, and autonomy. Far from being an idealistic activity, we are beginning to see that through the teaching of these skills children gain concrete understanding of the values of cooperation and interdependence that later can be extended to the world.

A MANUAL ON NONVIOLENCE AND CHILDREN is important in that it presents teachers with concrete ways for creating a classroom atmosphere in which children can gain the skills to solve their own conflicts. It can also lead to developing the kinds of thinking and behavior required for living peacefully in a tense world.

As adults we now have the responsibility to inspire in our children the determination and ability to resolve conflicts without the use of weapons. A world in which our children can become sophisticated in the skills of problem-solving, dialogue and negotiation is a world in which we are educating our children for survival.

—Paula J. Paul
Educators for Social Responsibility
Philadelphia, PA

A Manual on Nonviolence and Children

A NOTE FROM STEPHANIE . . .

Compiling and editing this manual has meant hours away from the office and from regular duties, from home, and sometimes from friends. I would like to thank the other members of the Peace Committee staff, especially my full-time office co-workers Marta Harrison and subsequently Lois Dorn, for their understanding, support, and humor. I worked in the attic study of "the gathering," and wish to thank the present members of that house for its use. Several friends, including Bruce Birchard and Demie Kurz, and my fellow house members at "Trollheim," especially Christopher Moore, gave me support and encouragement, which helped immensely.

Finally, I would like to appreciate myself, for sticking with it.

—Stephanie Judson

For the Fun of It!

APPRECIATIONS

In revising this handbook, and especially in writing the Foreword, I encountered frustrating obstacles, but the presence of real support and caring allowed me to finish in time for the last deadline.

In particular, I want to appreciate Joseph Kelemen, who continuously affirmed and supported me; Cynthia Arvio, who expressed her caring throughout the editing process; Ellen Deacon, whose thinking on excellence resurrected my thoughts from a year-old piece of writing; Jerry Kinchy, who generously offered his time and support in the layout work; Jim Lenhart, whose excitement generated more enthusiasm in me; Ruth Seeley, whose illustrations enrich the handbook with their beautiful, simple lines. I also want to thank Jennifer Haines, Mally Cox-Chapman, Stephanie Judson and Ellen Forsythe for their suggestions and affirming comments.

—Marta Harrison

Contents

Introduction

Creating an Atmosphere for Nonviolent Action

This manual is designed to help children and adults establish an *atmosphere* in which they can resolve their problems and conflict nonviolently. Therefore, it is a manual about action, or hard, joyful work.

Nonviolence is often associated with passivity, or "being nice" to the extent that somebody becomes a martyr or gets "walked over." But that is not what we mean by nonviolence. Here we mean nonviolent *action*; we mean ways that children and adults can act on the problems and challenges around them without emotionally or physically damaging anyone.

We make a firm assumption that people basically do not want to hurt each other. We also assume that everyone is capable of thinking about, and reacting creatively to, conflict. However, when people are overcome by fear, anger or other difficult feelings, when they have no sense of their own self-worth, no practice in looking for alternatives, they understandably find it hard to react creatively. Indeed, they may act violently under these conditions. Violence is a destructive reaction to conflict.

Following are five elements which we believe contribute to an atmosphere in which people can act nonviolently to resolve conflict.

1) Affirmation

Affirming somebody is acknowledging and appreciating good and admirable qualities in him or her. It is possible to find such qualities in every human being. Therefore, each person can be affirmed.

People need a sense of their own power and goodness, especially when dealing with difficult situations in their lives. Affirmation provides this, thereby helping us to think clearly and giving us the confidence to take creative action.

2) The Sharing of Feelings, Information, Experience

Sharing feelings with others breaks down the sense of isolation which keeps people from empathizing with others in conflict situations. It helps us to remember that at one time or another we have all been involved in conflict. Sharing feelings also allows us to work through past hurtful experiences and thus to see each conflict as a new situation for which a new response can be made.

In order to resolve a problem nonviolently, people need to have as much information as possible about the situation. Therefore, *sharing information* is important in empowering us to handle conflict.

Other people's experiences provide alternate models and approaches for us to consider in dealing with our own situations. By *sharing our own experiences* we get a chance to evaluate them and to draw out new insights to apply to the present.

3) Supportive Community

A supportive group atmosphere allows people to work together on problems and provides an ongoing confidence that "We can do it." In this atmosphere it is assumed that everyone has something to contribute and that everyone is part of the solution to conflict.

4) Problem-solving

Practice at solving problems builds confidence and skill. People who are practiced and confident can tackle difficult conflicts. Practice and confidence also help us pursue a problem until a workable solution is reached instead of giving up.

5) Enjoying Life

Beauty and joy are part of living. Delighting in beauty and celebrating joyfully keep people from being "bogged down" in problems. The less "bogged down" we are, the better we can think and act creatively about conflict.

We in the Nonviolence and Children Program believe that these elements help people to resolve conflict nonviolently; and further, we believe they nurture learning.

nonviolent action for adults and children fall under other categories (affirmation, sharing, community, enjoying living). If skills in these areas are well-developed, conflict will be reduced and more easily be handled. Therefore, most of the manual deals with these areas.

Especially for Adults

We are writing mostly for adults who are concerned about developing nonviolent attitudes and skills in children. We're writing for adults because they have tremendous power in children's lives and over children's facilities to handle conflict.

In fact, children may be in a better position than adults to deal with conflict nonviolently. First, children are able to take in a lot of information and to notice a great deal of detail in their environment which they can use in thinking about conflict. Second, because they haven't had as many years to build a negative self-image, children often have a better sense of self-worth and confidence than adults. Children have a shorter history of experiencing failure in handling conflict.

However, adults hold power to allow children either to build on their positive self-image or to establish a negative one. Adults can influence children to retain their ability to absorb information and detail. Adults can also interfere unnecessarily, inhibiting children's natural intelligence from operating freely to resolve a situation. We hope that this manual will help adults to nurture children's natural abilities in dealing with problems and conflict.

How This Manual
Approaches Conflict

In order to deal with conflict nonviolently, children and adults need tools and information which are not usually available to them. We attempt to make some of these tools and some of this information available here.

Yet only *one* section of the manual deals directly with problem-solving and conflict resolution. That is because most of the information and tools relevant to

2

Affirmation

> **Affirming somebody** is acknowledging and appreciating good and admirable qualities and abilities in him or her. It's possible to find such qualities in every human being. Therefore, every person can be affirmed.

Human beings, we believe, are naturally warm, loving, energetic and affirming. They want to help each other, work together, and share their strengths. Elise Boulding, a noted peace researcher, has found that people who work consistently to make positive changes in society have three characteristics in common: they are optimistic and competent, and have high self-esteem.* Moreover, these people are likely to be able to learn easily and to solve problems and resolve conflict well. Affirmation, which we believe comes naturally to human beings, is essential in nurturing these characteristics.

The Effects of Put-Downs

Unfortunately, ours is a "put-down" culture. We begin to experience negative criticism early in our lives. Children encounter a competitive grading system. Sarcasm and downgrading are common, even as signs of affection. Commercials, an outgrowth of a competitive society, encourage us to strive for their impossible standards. If we don't achieve these standards, we assume that we are "less-than-perfect" people.

This negative input understandably becomes ingrained in us. We begin to believe the direct or tacit criticism; we accept it as fact. For instance, in music class a teacher directs seven-year-old Sally to mouth the words without singing. Thirty years later, Sally shrugs resignedly: "I never could carry a tune." The list continues, for Sally and for others. "I just don't have a head for figures...am not the athletic type...not mechanically inclined...," etc.

With so much negative reinforcement, it is far easier to "give up" and to accept others' judgment than to struggle both against criticism and against the usual difficulties of learning new things. "Giving up" essentially means relinquishing the opportunity to learn as much as a human being is capable of learning, and relinquishing the power to make our own decisions about how we want our lives to be.

Although minority people receive more criticism than others, no one escapes entirely from put-downs and their effects. Even people who haven't encountered a lot of direct put-downs have been affected in some way by this negative atmosphere. For example, think of a friend or colleague whom you consider to be extremely capable, intelligent and confident. If you were to tell this person directly how you perceive him or her, he or she would most likely deny or laugh at some part of your affirmation. We have been so conditioned to think critically of ourselves that it is not possible to believe wholly in positive feedback.

The effect of put-downs, in summary, is twofold. First, they block learning. Second, they discourage people from being in control of their own lives, from solving their own problems, and from making changes for themselves. Since this negativity is such an all-pervasive part of our culture, we are all affected by it.

---

*Elise Boulding, "The Child and Nonviolent Social Change" in *Handbook on Peace Education*, Christoph Wulf, editor, Oslo: International Peace Research Association, 1974, pp. 101-132.

Affirmation and Learning

Learning is easiest when the learner feels relaxed and unthreatened. When we feel threatened or attacked, our response is either to lash back or to withdraw. Neither response allows information to enter our minds easily and to be assimilated.

In order to feel generally relaxed and unthreatened, we must feel confident in ourselves and in our abilities to learn. Then it is most possible for us to reach out into new areas and to explore them actively.

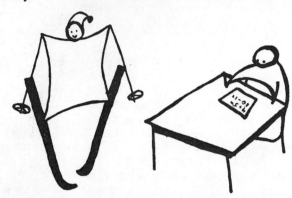

Affirmation builds confidence. Hearing that we are doing well, being creative and perceptive, grasping a problem and figuring it out, encourages us to continue to do so—to do so even more, and even better. When we begin to believe that we are learning well, and are able to hold onto that belief, we are able to affirm ourselves, and self-affirmation helps to continue to nurture the learning process.

Affirmation and Conflict Resolution

Feeling affirmed is a first step in conflict resolution. Having a sense of self-esteem makes it easier for us to see the good in others, including those with whom we are in conflict.

Moreover, if we know that we are liked and appreciated, conflict situations do not make us feel totally rejected, in spite of the tension on a particular issue or in a particular situation.

Just as affirmation helps a person to explore new information, it also helps an individual to reach for a variety of new alternatives to a conflict situation. A choice of alternatives helps to prevent destructive reactions to conflict, i.e., fighting back, freezing and not acting at all, or running away. Finally, having a sense both of self-worth and of alternatives establishes the opportunity not only to choose an alternative but to act on it.

4

Directed Affirmation Activities

An attitude of affirmation is always helpful. Wherever we are—in a classroom, at home, in a meeting, in a factory, getting dressed in the morning—we'll function best when we're appreciating ourselves and those around us.

There's no guaranteed way to establish or to maintain an atmosphere of affirmation. Each situation and person is different and requires some fresh thinking. Affirmation activities, when they are thoughtfully chosen and directed, can contribute to our efforts to create an understanding about the importance of affirmation. An affirmation activity may help to set a tone which catalyzes caring and support to develop outside the activity time. Affirmation activities may also provide a common experience of the kind of atmosphere which you as the facilitator can then expect and insist upon whenever the group is together.

It's important to remember, however, that affirmation *activities* are not crucial in establishing an affirming *atmosphere*. Maintaining an affirming attitude, being comfortable with and believing in affirmation, and thinking clearly about each individual in the group are the key elements in establishing an affirming atmosphere. An affirmation activity by itself, like any other technique, will not do this.

How to Set Up an Affirmation Activity

As the facilitator, you are important in the *process* of establishing and maintaining an affirming atmosphere in the group. Remember to enjoy the activities yourself and to use your own judgment!

Selecting an Activity

Think about what is appropriate for your group and the individuals in it. Some questions that it may be helpful to ask yourself are:

1) What do I want to accomplish in this group? How will this activity help?

2) Is the activity suitable for the level of trust in the group at the present time? Is it too threatening?

3) Is the activity open-ended enough to allow for individual expression?

4) Do I need to adapt the activity to the age group with which I am working? If so, how?

5) Do I feel comfortable with affirmation? How can I become more comfortable with it?

Presenting an Activity

Explain the importance of affirmation and the reasons for doing an affirmation activity. We all deserve an explanation of why we are asked to do something. The theory of affirmation and put-downs can be explained and understood by almost any age. When our explanations have been adapted to the language and experience of the age group, we've found that pre-schoolers through adults can easily understand. Moreover, given an explanation of affirmation, they are more willing to give it a try.

Explain the activity thoroughly before doing it, especially if it is new to the group. If needed, repeat the instructions as you proceed to each part of the activity.

The Power of the Put-Down: Explaining Affirmation Theory

We assume that anybody wants and deserves to know the reasons why he or she is asked to do something. This is certainly true for affirmation activities. If people understand the reasons for emphasizing affirmation, they are usually willing to give it a try.

One of the important concepts to explain is the power and pervasiveness of put-downs, or the negative remarks which permeate our everyday lives. Because they permeate, we're apt to be unaware of put-downs. So it is important to illustrate vividly how pervasive and how harmful put-downs are in order to persuade people to try to counter them.

Two approaches we have used with adults and children to illustrate this follow.

Brainstorming Put-Downs and Put-Ups

After a brief definition of what "put-downs" and "put-ups" (affirmations) are, the facilitator asks the group members to brainstorm all the put-downs and put-ups they can think of in, say, five minutes time. (Brainstorming is listing any idea or phrase that comes to mind, no matter how silly or wild or whatever. Nobody comments on anybody else's idea or phrase.)

The facilitator records the put-downs on a piece of flipchart paper or on one side of the blackboard, and the put-ups on another piece or on the other side of the board.

We have consistently found that the put-down list is longer than the put-up list; that it is much easier to think of the negative rather than the positive.

From here, the facilitator can go on to explain that:

1) We hear a lot of put-downs.

2) Put-downs hurt people. They stop us from learning and thinking.

3) We need to "fight put-downs" by being up front with affirmation, such as the kind of activities planned for today, or the next session.

IALAC Stands for
"I AM LOVEABLE AND CAPABLE"
Technique developed by Sidney B. Simon, affective educator

Each person, somewhere inside, has a belief that she or he *is* loveable and capable. But outside, lots of things contradict that belief, until the person begins to doubt it *inside*, too.

A good way of illustrating this is to use an IALAC sign. With IALAC (or something comparable) written on a piece of paper and taped to his or her chest, the facilitator explains to the group that he or she is a 7-year-old (or whatever appropriate age) starting out in the morning. What, asks the facilitator, are some of the comments that the 7-year-old person might hear?

For every put-down comment which somebody in the group suggests, the facilitator tears off a part of the paper IALAC sign. For every affirmation, the facilitator tapes a torn piece back onto the sign.

Using an IALAC sign this way dramatically illustrates the effect of put-downs and affirmations. It can also lead to informal discussion.*

Affirmation Activities

Opening and Closing Circle Affirmations

Warm physical contact with the whole group at the beginning and end of the day is an effective way to reduce put-downs and negativity, and to build affirmative community. The whole group can join together by holding hands or by linking arms to shoulders. Or people may just sit so everybody can see each other and can touch if they wish.

OPENING CIRCLE

Excitement-sharing: Each person recounts something new and good that has happened since the last time the group was together—something momentous, or (seemingly) small and trivial, that is going well and that she or he is pleased about (e.g., "My daddy came home last night. He'd been away for a week." "I smelled a rose on the way to school today.")

CLOSING CIRCLE

Closing circles can be a time to affirm oneself, others in the circle, and the whole group. The topics and variations are endless; here are a few:

1) Name the type of flower, animal, tree, etc., which the person on your left and/or right reminds you of and tell why. (E.g., "Sarah, you remind me of a gazelle, because you think in graceful leaps. Joe, you strike me as a pheasant or a rainbow trout, because you dress so colorfully.")

2) Take some quality you like about the person on your left for your own; give one of your positive qualities to the person on your right (e.g., "Gerald, I'd like to have your knowledge of and caring for animals. Michele, I'll give you my bravery to do something even when I'm scared.")

3) Say a word, or two or three, which express your feelings about being with the group (appropriate when it's been an especially good time together) (e.g., warm, tender, thoughtful, delighted, glowing, supportive; happy, groovy, "snarfy," bouncy, "I like it.")

4) Tell "What I've appreciated about you lately." The group should be small (up to six or so). Each person is affirmed by the others and then takes time to affirm herself or himself. In a large group, the facilitator may ask for two or three appreciations only for each person.

5) Standing in a circle, sing a song everyone knows.
   or
   Play a simple game together.
   or
   Pass a hand squeeze or a hug around the circle (see Games, p. G-26).

In the Teachers' Lounge...

One clever teacher instituted excitement-sharing in the teachers' lounge of her school. Now, instead of the usual griping about "those kids," teachers have agreed to enter the lounge by exclaiming or sharing about something which pleased them. The atmosphere of the lounge—and of the teachers' social time together—has radically changed.

---

* A longer description of the "IALAC" technique is available in Sidney Simon's *I Am Loveable and Capable*. For information on ordering this write to Argus Communications, 7440 Natchez Avenue, Niles, Illinois 60648.

Active Affirmation Games

There are several cooperative games which are very affirming, and others which can be adapted to be so. Four in particular are:

GESTURE NAME GAME (see Games, p. G-8). It's affirming to act out your own name and then to have your motions and name repeated twice.

I'M GOING ON A TRIP. Instead of taking along a toothbrush and a pair of pants for this memory game, take along something you like about yourself, and a gesture of physical affection (see Games, p. G-12).

QUALITY INITIALS (see Games, p. G-9). A truly self-affirming game!

INVENT YOUR OWN affirmation game. "Catch a Falling Star," a delightful game created to celebrate Marta Harrison, indicates the potential for many more affirmation games (see Games, pp. G-22,23).

Written Affirmations

Affirmations often do not sink in the first time they are spoken. Written affirmations provide a lasting record to be returned to, and referred to, again and again. Since the affirmations are both spoken and written, they also reinforce reading skills.

AFFIRMATION SILHOUETTES
Description: Each person has a piece of butcher paper or newsprint about a foot longer than she or he is tall. People pair up (adults included) and take turns tracing each other full-length on the Paper with marking pens. They can decorate the silhouettes as realistically or imaginatively as they wish, immediately or later on, as time allows.

Then about two people per session stand in front of the group while everyone takes a turn to say a positive, affirming thing directly to that person. Finally, the person in front of the group affirms himself or herself.

Meanwhile, someone who writes quickly records the affirmations on a sheet of paper. This affirmation sheet goes to the person at the end of his or her turn. Later on, each affirmation is written on a separate index card and pasted onto the silhouette. The finished product is posted where everyone can see.

Materials:
butcher paper or newsprint
magic markers and/or crayons
assorted materials for decorating silhouettes
index cards
paste

Thoughts: This has been an important tool for families, Sunday schools, faculties, as well as children in classrooms. We use it when enough trust has been built up. Take well-liked people first, and always explain the importance of affirmation before the exercise begins.

Nevertheless, it is a difficult task for some children. It's embarrassing to counter all the usual put-downs. Unwritten classroom laws (e.g., "Boys never say anything nice to girls.") add to the difficulty. The teacher or facilitator must decide the sincerity of what's said. "I like your red sneakers." may be what the child has available at the moment. The tone of what's said is more important than what is actually stated.

For participants having a really difficult time thinking of anything to say, it may be helpful to be asked specific questions: "Is there something you like to do together?" "What's something you've seen Johnny do well?" It's important to *wait* for the child to have time to think.

7

Variations on Silhouettes

Teachers have been creative and ingenious in adapting affirmation silhouettes for their own uses. Two adaptations follow:

Lynne Vlaskamp, a kindergarten teacher at Moorestown Friends School, decided that she did not have enough wall space in her classroom for full-body silhouettes. Instead, she used a filmstrip projector to trace students' heads. She cut out two identical profiles of each student, one copy on white construction paper, the other on black. The black profile, pasted onto a colorful piece of paper, went home with each child as a Mother's Day present. The white profile, also mounted on a piece of construction paper, was posted on a bulletin board in the classroom.

Each day during circle time, a kindergartner had a turn to be affirmed. Lynne explained that this was the time for everyone to share something that he or she liked about the person. She recorded the comments directly onto the white profile; children took their profiles home at the end of the year.

At first, children were hesitant to have a turn. Soon, however, they were eager to have a chance. Parents who came for end-of-the-year conferences were amazed. "Do the others really feel that way about my child?" Some children even tried to repeat the process at home. "So that's what Susie was trying to do when she wanted to trace my head!"

Lynne found this a good vehicle for discussing with parents the importance of affirmation and feelings of self-worth.

The Nonviolence and Children Program staff did affirmation silhouettes with Dorothy Lenk and her sixth grade students at Lansdowne Friends School (see p.57). The following year Dorothy, a skilled photographer, took pictures of each of her students. Instead of having the class make full-length silhouettes, Dorothy enlarged the pictures and mounted the students' affirmations around them. This was Dorothy's graduation present to her students at the end of the year.

Appreciating Colleagues

The other day I asked myself, "When was the last time you appreciated another teacher, out loud, to the person?" I realized it had been quite a while. It's easy enough to do that with a child. But teachers need it just as much.

—*Craig Putnam*

YEAR-ROUND VALENTINES

Description: After giving some thought to the child, the adult writes an affirming note, then leaves the "valentine" under the child's pillow, in his or her desk during recess, or wherever it may easily be discovered.

Materials: assorted paper construction materials, a card, etc.

Thoughts: Since "valentines" can be made during a quiet, reflective moment, they provide a chance to think carefully about the person being affirmed. It is a good time to appreciate a person for the areas in which she or he is developing, as well as those in which the person is already doing well.

In one classroom, the teacher wrote two or three valentines each day. She placed them in students' desks during recess. The students soon caught on and raced back at the end of recess to see who was affirmed that day.

After a while, students began writing valentines to their teacher, providing the affirmation which every teacher needs. Finally, the students spontaneously started writing valentines to each other.

BIRTHDAY NOTEBOOKS

Description: Each person has a sheet of notebook paper on which to write and/or draw affirmations of the birthday person. The sheets are put together into a looseleaf notebook for presentation at the birthday celebration.

Materials:

looseleaf notebook
paper for each participant
crayons, pencils, etc.

Thought: This can be used to celebrate a person on any special occasion, not just a birthday.

"Whenever I'm feeling down, I'm going to read this book out loud, and loudly!" Christopher Moore, upon receiving his birthday notebook.

I'M GREAT BOOK

Description: The "I'm Great Book" consists of several dittoed sheets oriented around self-affirmation. (Some samples are included here. The variations are endless—you can make up your own.)

Each dittoed sheet is handed out at an appropriate time (probably best not all at once, though the classroom or group may be structured so that it's appropriate to have the sheets available for the time when a person is ready to use them).

The facilitator explains the instructions, which are written here at the bottom of each sheet.

When all the sheets are completed, they are bound together into a special cover created by the "author."

Materials:

dittoed sheets for each person
pencils and crayons or something to color with
materials for durable covers (such as oaktag or posterboard)
something to fasten sheets and cover together (brass fasteners work well)

Note: The "I'm Great Book" is Sarah Putnam's adaptation for her second grade class of the "Affirmation Notebook," developed by Quaker Project on Community Conflict in New York.* Sarah intends to add sheets which would require children to work together. One example might be a sheet which had several interviewing questions for a child to use in interviewing a friend. Another is a sheet which a child and parent would fill out together.

What sheets would you add? Let us know if you come up with some.

T-Shirt

Write your name on the shirt.

Write one or two words that describe you.

Draw a picture on it of something you like to do.

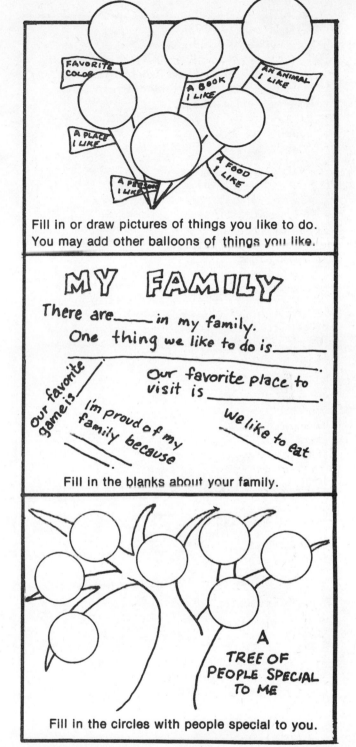

Fill in or draw pictures of things you like to do. You may add other balloons of things you like.

MY FAMILY

There are _____ in my family.
One thing we like to do is _____.

Our favorite game is _____

Our favorite place to visit is _____.

I'm proud of my family because _____.

We like to eat _____

Fill in the blanks about your family.

A TREE OF PEOPLE SPECIAL TO ME

Fill in the circles with people special to you.

Note to teacher: This modified "family tree" may include parents, siblings, aunts, uncles, cousins, friends, pets, etc. There is no one circle for mother, for example, and it may be appropriate to emphasize that there is no "right" or "normal" family.

* There is a more detailed account of "Affirmation Notebooks" in *A Handbook* of the Children's Creative Response to Conflict Program. Order from Quaker Project on Community Conflict, 15 Rutherford Place, New York, NY 10003. $5.00 plus postage and handling includes the handbook and a one-year subscription to the project's newsletter. The handbook alone costs $3.50 plus postage and handling.

Taking a Risk

I've heard and believed that "around the circle" affirmation, where a child has a chance to be affirmed by others in the circle, should be done only after other affirmation activities and lead-up exercises have built up a feeling of trust, security and caring among the children.

Last fall I was reading a story with my class about a girl who was saying that she was a pretty great person. When we discussed the story, some children said she was bragging. I remarked that perhaps that was so, but she could also just be feeling really good about herself. I continued by explaining that it was important for us all to feel good about ourselves. I asked them to think about something really nice about themselves. Then they each had a turn to share their thoughts. I was pleased—this was a good beginning affirmation activity and fit right into the flow of things.

All but one child thought of something good. The exception was a wonderful, well-liked girl who has tremendous lack of self-confidence. She just couldn't think of anything nice about herself.

I knew I hadn't done the preliminary work, but I decided that the situation was important enough to take a risk. So we went around the circle, with each child saying something good about this girl. It worked fantastically. The children said wonderful things, and the girl was surprised, and thrilled.

—Karen Snyder

On the Subway

One day when I was waiting for a subway, a woman and two children sat down beside me. The baby sat happily in her lap; the young boy stood looking around curiously at signs and lights and tracks and flashing numbers. He asked his mother what the numbers were, what subway they were waiting for, when would it come, what did the red light mean, the yellow light, how would they know where it would stop, was that a #13 or a #34 subway...???

At first she answered his questions willingly and thoughtfully, but she soon started to lose patience. She distracted him with cookies, gave curt and repetitive answers, and scolded him to "Sit down, sit down." The next thing I knew she was telling him that he wouldn't be able to stay up when they got home.

I sat there through all this really wanting to say something to her but wasn't sure what. It suddenly occurred to me to affirm her child's questions and her own good answers. As I silently practiced the words I might use, their subway came and they left. I had some sense of 'missing an opportunity,' but that was outweighed by a sense of knowing what I would do 'next time.' It was exciting to think about using affirmation this way.

—Karen Zaur

Having an Effect...

We can have a strong effect simply by sharing with another adult the positive things we notice about a child. Last summer I worked in a reform school. When I noticed some positive thing in a child, I'd try to bring it up in a staff meeting or in conversation with the other staff. There certainly was enough negative stuff flying around.

I didn't know, though, how much effect it had on the children until one boy came up to me, remarking, "I heard what you said about me in staff meeting."

My remarks sometimes seemed to give a child more hope, more space, a new beginning; sometimes an adult was willing to see the child in a new light and that made a lot of difference.

—Sue Bowden

Resistance to Affirmation

What Happens If ...?

When conscious, consistent affirmation is introduced into a group, some people are likely to be uncomfortable. The spontaneous affirmations seem "unreal" to them and the affirmation activities "hokey" or downright distasteful.

It's understandable that they feel this way. After years of societal conditioning and resultant peer pressure against openly affirming much of anything, of course they feel uncomfortable when they hear good things about themselves and others.

It's not that these good things aren't true, but only that we've been told otherwise for so long that it's hard to hear the positive.

But even though people may be uncomfortable, it still makes sense to continue your efforts. And there are ways you can help people to get past their discomfort and resistance.

Signs of Resistance

People indicate their discomfort in several ways. Here is a list of some which you may find as you affirm someone or as the group is participating in an affirmation activity.

— talking loudly or nervously.
— "blanking out," not being able to think of anything affirming to say.
— wriggling around or making nervous gestures (e.g., clicking pens, tapping fingernails).
— staring out the window, into space, or any place except at the person being affirmed or doing the affirming.
— openly declaring, "I don't want to do it," or protesting, "Do I have to?" "I have a stomach ache." "Is participating mandatory?" and so forth.
— screeching, teasing, etc., particularly focused on male/female relationships. This happens most frequently with upper elementary school and junior high students but is almost never absent.

Actually, these signs of resistance are unknowing requests to release the feelings and tension that come from hearing all that affirmation. But the signs themselves don't release the tension of the feelings.

Helping to Release Tension

Some physical actions which *do* release tension are:

— giggling, laughing
— perspiring, e.g., damp hot or cold clammy hands
— shaking, shivering
— tears, crying, sobbing
— yawning

Unlike signs of resistance, these actions actually can help people to release their feelings about affirmation and to "hear" affirmation better.

Just as there is societal conditioning against affirmation, there is also societal pressure not to release feelings physically, i.e., not to laugh too hard, not to show fear by shaking, or not to cry. The facilitator can help to counter that pressure by making it safe enough for people to feel that it's okay to release the tension which they are feeling.

Here are some elements in building the necessary safety for the release of tension.

1) When you notice that participants actually are releasing tension, e.g., by giggling, shivering, etc., explain to the whole group that this is normal, natural and healthy. Insist that nobody ridicule this behavior; making fun stops the normal, helpful process of release.

2) Be sensitive to how much release at the time of the exercise is appropriate and does not get in the way of what else is happening. For instance, during an affirmation activity the person whose turn it is to be affirmed may feel uncomfortable or "put-down" by giggles. If so, give the giggles a chance to come out beforehand, and then ask that they stop during the affirmation.

3) Realize that there are some affirmation exercises which require more understanding and safety than others. It is important to be sensitive to the needs and capacities of the people in your group. Begin with activities which people can do easily, and build from there. By proceeding slowly, work towards helping participants be more comfortable with affirmation as an everyday, normal "fact of life."

4) Examine how you yourself feel about affirming and being affirmed. The group will take its cues from you. If you can affirm yourself and others easily, accept affirmation from others, release tension yourself and accept others' doing so, the group will have a good model. You will be an inspiration to them of a warm, loving, energetic, affirming human being.

11

Use of Laughter

I think the thing that gets in the way of children really caring for one another in the classroom is their embarrassment. Embarrassment encompasses self-consciousness, fear of being wrong, of making a fool of oneself. When I think of embarrassment, I think of things like a child's being so self-conscious that she or he can't think. A very shy child can't remember her name. Other children can't think of a caring thing to say to each other.

Laughter seems to drain a whole lot of the punch from embarrassment. We have begun structuring situations to allow more laughter. Stephanie and I were working with a very fine fourth grade, beginning the affirmation portraits. A girl was being affirmed, and all the girls in the class had affirmed her. The boys were hedging. (There was a strong "boy vs. girl" ethic in the class.) I picked a boy to come up. He did, took one look at the girl and began to crack up, protesting, "I can't do it!" All the other boys were holding in their laughter through blue lips. I gave everybody permission to laugh, and for about 90 seconds there was good solid laughter. The boys proceeded to finish the affirmation with no difficulty.

—*Keith Miller*

A Memo on Different Types of Affirmation

I have noticed that there are three different categories of affirmation. First, there's factual affirmation, or saying good things which we know to be true about the person we're talking to. For instance, you may have been told a hundred times that you have beautiful brown eyes. Though you may wish that someone would find something else to enjoy about you, it's still good to hear you have beautiful brown eyes.

In the second kind of affirmation, the affirmer is actually asking for attention for himself or herself from the person he or she is affirming. Sometimes adults and children slip into this kind of affirmation without noticing. They say things such as, "You are really nice to be around when you're quiet," or, "I sure feel good when you say nice things to me." To test for this, add the words, "I feel," to the sentence. It will usually still make sense.

This is not a bad kind of affirmation. It does affirm the other person. However, we must be clear that we are really asking for attention for our own feelings. This may be inappropriate, or even manipulative, if we are intending to give full attention to the person being affirmed.

In the third type of affirmation, we affirm a person in the area in which he or she really needs to be affirmed at that very moment. This will be different every time. For instance, when a student who generally has a hard time with math puts up his or her hand and tries to offer a solution, we might say, "You are very alert today." The student may not *feel* alert and may deny that this kind of affirmation is "true." But we are affirming abilities and qualities, not the feelings of inferiority or incompetence.

This third kind of affirmation may bring feelings to the surface, and the person being affirmed may squirm, laugh, cry, or in some other way physically release the feelings. This is fine and actually helps the person to think more clearly about the math problem and to believe that he or she *is* alert.

—*Chuck Esser*

A Headstart Center

Where Nobody Is Allowed to Put Anybody Down

by Sarah Taylor
Lambertville, N.J., Headstart
April, 1976

Two years ago I took a job as director of a Headstart center. Headstart's big emphasis is to educate parents, believing that they're the people who have a prime influence on a child's life. Except for the nurse and the director, the people who work there are supposed to be parents whose children are in, or who have been in, Headstart.

I really agree with the emphasis on educating parents. But when I first took the job, I found a staff that wasn't doing this. My center is in a small town where families have feuded for generations. The staff for the most part was made up of people who had worked there for a long time, had age-old antagonisms toward each other, and were in poor emotional and physical health.

I knew that I had to "clean the basement," because the staff was hurting both the children and the parents through its own state of affairs. By "cleaning the basement," I don't mean that I intended to fire anybody. I intended to make people feel better about themselves.

So the first year I concentrated on the staff. I explained that we'd start our staff meetings with self-affirmations. I took every opportunity to encourage affirmations, verbalizing what was good, pleasing, exciting—anything positive in their lives. I made one rule: Nobody is allowed to put anybody down, including herself.

It was a good thing that I was boss. That's the only reason at first that the staff agreed to do any of this. "If the boss says I have to, I guess I'll do it." But it was contrary to anything that they'd ever experienced. They felt that positive things were not only hard to say, they were almost immoral. Christians didn't do that kind of thing. And besides, they weren't true. So it was scary for me to keep on insisting that we do it. But after awhile, it caught on. People even came back from their summer vacations saying, "I've been thinking what my 'good' experience is about my vacation, because I knew you'd ask."

The Federal Government required evaluations of each staff person. So I began by writing really positive things about each one. I showed each staff person what I'd written; they couldn't believe that anybody would say those things about them. Then I asked each person to write up her own evaluation and insisted that she put in a lot of positive things. After all this, we'd talk about areas that the person needed to grow in. People were accurate about themselves—they usually are, I think—and if they know they've done a lot of positive stuff, it isn't hard to talk about growing in other ways. Finally, we'd set goals for each person—maybe going to a special workshop or visiting another Headstart center.

The government wouldn't accept oooperative evaluations with a lot of different writing on them. The first forms we sent got returned. So now we type up the final form after everything is done—but the cooperative process is still the same.

I kept on enforcing the "no put-down" rule. Maybe there's a reason for you to be late, sloppy sometimes, sleepy. That's OK. But there's no reason for anybody to put anybody else down.

The second year, I began to teach conflict resolution. I figured that we wouldn't be effective in responding to conflict with the children if there were two staff people whom the children loved who weren't speaking to each other. What kind of sense would that make to the children? But there sure were long-term hatreds among the staff members. I would sit two people down, insist that they affirm themselves and each other, and then ask them to say what was really on their minds and hearts about each other. That was scary, but so important! Certainly staff members can't help children resolve their conflicts until they have worked on their own.

The second year I really concentrated on the parents, too. I've been doing a lot of home visits, trying to do the same affirming things. I found that the parents believed that the sign of a good parent was putting their children down in order to "keep them in their place" so they wouldn't get swelled heads. A good parent puts down a child as part of a code of ethics.

13

I insisted again. "We're not allowed to talk that way in Headstart." Those parents are all bigger than I am. I held my breath. They must have been saying to themselves, "Oh, yeah? Oh yes we are!" But I was the director, so they kept their mouths shut. Later, when I'd remind them about that rule, they would remember and seem to accept it. And once they accepted the fact that it was a rule, they began to internalize it.

At the center, we cleaned and painted a tiny boiler room and made it into a parent's room. That was their place to sit around, talk, meet, smoke, socialize. Parents began to come. On any given day now there are about six mothers who would rather die than not come, and maybe four others who join them. That's pretty good for a center serving 23 children. There are programs for parents now, too. Once a week, a psychologist comes to talk with them; and there is also a weekly nutrition class, an exercise class, and a film series and discussion group up the river from us a ways. We've focused on different things from time to time, too, such as crafts, a few sessions on alcoholism, obesity, etc.

Most Headstart centers require that the parents volunteer some time. Indeed, many of the parents in my center do volunteer. But I made it clear that it was fine if they wanted to sit and talk. They just had to follow our only rule: they couldn't put each other down.

I really encouraged physical touching and affection. I hugged a lot, and, of course, still do. One day recently a community aide came up to me and said, "Here's a hug for the person who taught me how to hug."

They became more comfortable with touching each other. I really encouraged it, hugging anybody who I thought could take it. Usually there was at least one parent who was open to hugging and affection, and I did a lot of accidental bumping into people with whom I was a little frightened to be openly affectionate.

The parents know that it is a strain to be at home alone with a really small child 24 hours a day. Now they realize that it's not necessary; they can come to the center. One day a small child, too young to be in Headstart, was in the parent's room without his mother. One of the "regulars" asked, "Whose baby is that?" Another remarked, "Oh, it doesn't matter, they're all the same; we're all a family."

I'm doing well at Headstart. We all are.

Thoughts on Sarah Taylor's Work

When I was teaching school, I noticed the strange dichotomy between the really fantastic teaching and the truly caring attitude that the staff members had toward the children on the one hand, and the pervasive negative, political atmosphere in the relations among the staff members on the other. There were a lot of bad vibrations and secrecy and rumors having to do with hiring, firing, and the power structure of the school. Moreover, the teachers were keenly aware of the politics among the parents over the school and of the difficulties within families, divorces and such.

We really did care about and love the children. And yet the children weren't really enjoying the school. I wonder if this wasn't because of all the other negative stuff that seemed to pervade the atmosphere. We tried to counter negatives in and among the children, but not among the adults. That must have affected the children.

—From a participant in a small group discussion, after listening to Sarah Taylor's account of her work at Headstart

14

Sarah Taylor's eloquent description of her work in Headstart is an appropriate conclusion for this section. Look what can happen when we adopt a mindset of affirmation! Here, it really led to conflict resolution.

Once again, we wish to emphasize that affirmation activities by themselves will not "do the trick." Used thoughtfully, they contribute to a more whole understanding and an attitude of affirmation.

Envision what affirmation might lead to in your own situation, with your family, students, peers, colleagues...*yourself*.

REFERENCES AND RESOURCES
FOR AFFIRMATION

Harvey Jackins, "Nature of the Learning Process," Rational Island Publishers, P.O. Box 2081, Main Office Station, Seattle, Washington 98111. $.50.

An exposition of much of the theory and assumptions which the Nonviolence and Children Program uses.

Marianne Simon, "Chasing Killer Statements from the Classroom," *Learning Magazine*, August/September 1975, pp. 79-84.

A succinct and readable account of how to communicate affirmation theory in the classroom, how to reduce put-downs and increase put-ups.

Jack Canfield and Howard Wells, *100 Ways to Enhance Self-Concept in the Classroom*, Prentice-Hall, Englewood Cliffs, N.J., 1976. $11.95 hardback, $5.95 paperback.

A well-compiled and visually pleasing book which has, indeed, over 100 affirmative activities.

Sharing

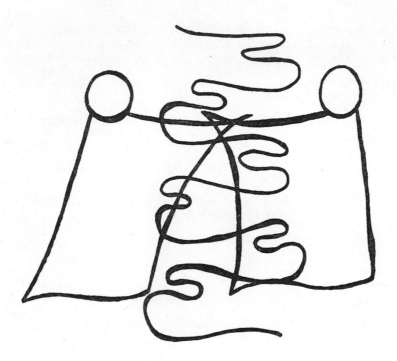

Young children often express themselves easily and spontaneously. They run up to share their excitement with anybody who will listen. They will seek somebody they feel safe with and cry out the feelings about something that has upset them. They construct play situations to explore and to share experiences, new information, and ideas.

How do we encourage sharing to continue as children become older? How do we find ways to share easily ourselves?

Sharing breaks down the strong sense of loneliness and isolation in our culture. Breaking it down enables us to work together towards resolving common problems and conflicts and to enjoy celebrating life together.

Sharing Feelings

Learning and acting effectively are significantly connected to emotions. Students cannot pay full attention to a reading lesson if they are upset about a pet dying or about an argument at home. Teachers cannot easily observe their students' progress if they are annoyed with their class's behavior or frustrated with administrative bureaucracy. Parents cannot nurture and care for their children well when they are arguing constantly with each other or continually worried about finances.

Having somebody pay attention to us while we share our feelings helps us to deal with our emotions so that we can learn and act effectively.

Sharing Experiences

Good friends often share experiences spontaneously and in detail. Many children, especially young ones, will approach a friendly listener to recount what is on their minds. There is a human need to talk about what is happening to us and often to describe or even release our feelings.

We learn from doing this. We explore our common and different experiences and gain a deeper understanding and appreciation of each other. Being able to talk freely about our experiences allows us to sort out the feelings involved and may also lead to actual release of feelings. Thus, we can evaluate the situation emotionally as well as rationally which helps us to see it in perspective.

Sharing Information and Ideas

Having information often comes with having power. People "in power" frequently hold information which they do not make available to others. Therefore, sharing or exchanging information can mean distributing power instead of allowing it to remain with a few people.

The Watergate affair is a good example of this in United States history. When the information about the actions of Nixon and some of his staff became widely available, a broad base of public opinion made it necessary for him to resign. Neither the strength of the individuals nor the authority of their offices could withstand the power of the people once they had the information.

In the classroom, many teachers grade or evaluate their students according to specific criteria. Teachers may keep these criteria to themselves, or they may share it with their students. By sharing the information, the teacher distributes some power in the grading system to the students. The students can hold the teacher to his or her word on how the system will work. The students can also choose whether to orient their work toward the teacher's criteria in order to receive a higher grade.

Having information also gives us an increased ability to understand human interactions. Small children can be very frightened and threatened by people laughing loudly at something they don't understand and may assume that the laughter is directed at them. If somebody explains why people are laughing, the children are freed to ignore the hilarity or to join in.

Sharing information and ideas can build a group's power to solve problems. For instance, in the "goal-wish problem-solving process" (see Conflict Resolution, p. 44) one person's ideas may spark another's thinking and yield a variety of alternatives to a problem.

Sharing information can also be helpful in resolving conflicts between two people or within a group of people. If people in conflict can share information on how they *feel* about a difficult situation, or how they each perceive what happened to cause the conflict, they are often able to reduce the level of tension among them. Then they can move more readily to resolve the conflict.

Strong feelings often prevent people from sharing information. Once these feelings are released or put aside enough for information to be shared, a solution can often be found to the conflict.

Understanding Feelings

The Nonviolence and Children Collective has been operating from some basic assumptions about people and about feelings. These assumptions undergird our work, and operate throughout the manual. We attempt to consolidate them below.

- People of all ages are phenomenally intelligent. We have the capacity to think and act creatively in any situation.*

- Bad feelings (anger, fear, sadness, embarrassment, guilt, feelings of inadequacy, shyness) are our responses to past or present experiences of being hurt.

- Such feelings are not thinking. In fact, feelings can interfere with both logical and intuitive thinking. (Intuition is an important concept. Not all thinking is carefully reasoned out and structured. In fact, some of our best thinking results from hunches or flashes of insight. We may say "I feel this is right," when we actually mean "I intuit," or "I have a sense that this is right.")

- Our feelings are not us. Neither good nor bad feelings alone give an accurate picture of our basic human nature. However, if nobody pays attention to our feelings, they begin to seem to be us. (How easy it is, for example, to assume that we *are* stupid because a particular situation is making us *feel* stupid!)

- When somebody is giving loving and warm attention to a person having strong feelings, that person will frequently release the feelings by crying, shaking, raging, laughing, yawning, and talking. This is easy to observe in small children, or in an older person who is in the midst of a very upsetting situation.

- Releasing emotion this way is a healthful, human process. It results in a "clearing of the head" so that we can mobilize our abilities to think and act well.

Once we recognize the difference between our intelligent, thinking selves and our feelings, it is possible to decide what to do in a particular situation and to act, regardless of what we are feeling. If at the earliest opportunity, we find a caring person who will listen to us awarely while we unload those feelings that were set aside, the feelings will be less likely to interfere in the future.

Allowing and encouraging feelings to be released will affect what happens next. One teacher recounts, "When Joey first came to school last fall, he cried for a whole week. I just carried him around and let him cry most of the time. After that he was fine, and he's having a great first year!" Another version of the story is all too familiar. "That George! He got off on the wrong foot this year, whining and wanting to go home, and I've had problem after problem. If he isn't tugging on me for attention, he's bothering another child who's trying to work, or he's making a mess!"

Sometimes it's not possible to encourage others to unload their feelings. The environment may not be conducive to it, or perhaps we ourselves are not prepared to pay attention while somebody releases feelings. In these cases, it is helpful to change the tone of things, taking attention away from the feelings for awhile and providing space for people to begin thinking again. Suggesting some quick activity (see Attention Out Activities, p. G-20) or a chance to appreciate each other may be appropriate at these times.

---

* Actual damage to the forebrain does reduce intelligence. However, this is not to be confused with the recent faddish concern with MBD, "Minimal Brain Damage." Actual brain damage often appears to be highly questionable when somebody is labelled with MBD.

Some Thoughts on
Sharing Activities

Structured Activities Are Helpful

We all have abilities to communicate well with other people about our feelings, our experiences, and information we hold. But often an aware listener is not available, and there are strong social messages that it is weak, silly, or bothersome to want to communicate. Thus inhibitions get built up against developing and using our natural abilities.

We are born, also, with great potential for listening. With increased years and learning, our ability grows. We can give close attention to anything or anyone we choose. Difficulties arise primarily because we also need to be listened to. If nobody listens to us, we are less free to listen well to others.

Structured activities which allow us to exercise our abilities to communicate and to listen can help us recover these capacities. The purpose of these activities is to make spontaneous interactions easier, not to replace them. The activities should be used thoughtfully, and never coercively. For instance, the teacher or facilitator should never ask a group to do something which she or he is not willing to do.

The activities which follow may be included in daily situations or used as part of working through conflict. As such, they are valuable tools.

The Right to Pass

In all sharing activities, everybody has the right to pass. Nobody must ever be *forced* to speak about thoughts, ideas, or personal feelings. This guideline, like all others, should be stated at the beginning of a sharing activity.

There are often varied and complex motives for opting to pass. The topic may be so personal or troubling that the individual may choose not to share it with the group. He or she may feel "tongue-tied" at the moment. Perhaps he may feel as if he is protecting somebody else, perhaps she may feel as if she is protecting herself. Maybe she feels that nobody would understand or that her thoughts may be misconstrued. He may be daydreaming or thinking about something else.

Many of the reasons for wishing to pass have to do with safety. For one reason or another, it doesn't feel safe enough right now to take a turn.

The facilitator is in a key position to present the right to pass as a dignified, acceptable option. The question for the facilitator is not, "How can we *make* him or her talk?" but, "Is there anything that I or we can do to make it safer for this person?"

Sharing Activity Guidelines

- **Each person, including the teacher or facilitator, gets a turn to share.**

- **No one has to speak. Everyone has the right to pass.**

- **No one speaks or comments during another person's turn, because people feel less safe to talk about experiences or feelings when they know they might be interrupted.**

19

Sharing Activities

Introductions and Interviews

Children in a classroom, teachers on a faculty, or any group of people who work together will function best if they know each other well. Introductions are useful at the beginning of the group's time together. Different types of introductions and interviews throughout the time together will help, too.

Interviews and introductions which include affirming questions can encourage people to think about themselves in positive and creative ways. This helps to create a supportive group identity and helps participants believe in themselves and in the group. Participants become proud to be group members and eager to help the group function well.

ACTIVE INTRODUCTION GAMES

There are several introduction games which get people moving, laughing and enjoying each other. Some are described on pages G8-10.

PAIRED INTRODUCTIONS

People in the group divide into pairs to interview each other for about three to five minutes. A prepared list of open-ended questions on the board or on a large piece of paper is helpful. While one person in the pair responds to the questions, the other listens carefully, commenting only to draw out the talker or to clarify information. They then switch roles, giving the listener the same chance to talk.

Each person then introduces his or her partner to the whole group, using the information gained in the interview. (People may want to take notes during the interview if they think they might forget things about their partners. That way, they can listen to other people being introduced without worrying whether they'll remember their information.)

Materials: wall charts or blackboard to write down prepared questions for the whole group to refer to.

20

Sample questions:

- What's your full name? Are you named after anybody?
- Who is a person you admire in history?
- If you could go anywhere and do anything you'd like to do tomorrow, where would you go and what would you do?
- If you could live sometime in the past or in the future, when would you choose to live? Why?

To the facilitator: Paired introductions let everybody get involved right away. That helps to build group warmth quickly and gives each individual some affirming attention.

Prepared open-ended questions help people begin talking with each other. They provide something to hang on to. But if participants want to "just talk," that's fine, too. The questions are to be helpful, not confining.

As the facilitator you should think ahead of time about which questions would be appropriate for that particular group.

NAMETAGS

Bright, colorful nametags are fun to make. They're also an easy way for people to learn each other's names. At several Nonviolence and Children workshops, we've noticed that a table full of assorted construction paper, glue, paste, yarn, scissors, etc., will draw arriving people together as they create celebrations of their names. Younger children feel free to return to the table when they need a break from too much talking and sitting.

INTERVIEW

Each person (but maybe not all on the same day) gets a chance to be interviewed in front of the group by the teacher or facilitator, who asks open-ended questions about various aspects of the person's life, orienting the questions to the level and interests of the person being interviewed.

Sometimes the facilitator invites questions from the interviewee, making the interview a two-way process. Sometimes questions from the rest of the group are invited. Sometimes the interviewee may ask to be interviewed on a particular topic.

On any question, the interviewee always has the right to pass. The facilitator or the interviewee can end the interview at any time by saying, "Thank you for the interview" and shaking hands, or in some other friendly way indicating closure.

Sample Prepared Questions

Appropriate vital statistics: What's your name? Where do you live?

Questions from the past: What's something you liked to do when you were younger (for instance, for sixth graders, when you were five years old)?

Questions from the present: What do you like to do in your free time? What's an important hobby for you?

A question from the fantasy realm: If you could do anything for one day, and had as much money as you needed, what would you do?

Questions about work: What's interesting to you in school? What's something you can teach really well?

A question to focus attention on the present: What's something in this room that you'd like to look at more closely?

To the facilitator: Interviewing is especially useful for groups of children or adults who aren't ready to handle a paired introduction format. It also allows appropriate questions, tailor-made for each individual.

The interview should be kept fairly short (about five minutes, and shorter for younger children). As the facilitator, you can judge the group's attention span. If you're interviewing somebody alone without the group, the length of the interview depends on the two of you.

With practice, you will become more and more adept at interviewing. The best questions are often the spontaneous ones that occur to you right in the process of the interview, as you are paying attention and learning about the person you're interviewing.

There is an excellent description of the interview process in *Values Clarification, a Handbook of Practical Strategies for Teachers and Students*, by Sidney Simon, et. al.*

ROUND ROBIN INTERVIEW

People roam around the room for 10-15 minutes, interviewing each other. Each person gets to speak with several others. It is helpful to jot down notes during the interview so that the information can be recalled when the group reconvenes.

The facilitator calls the group back together, and invites one person to come up in front of the group. The facilitator asks this person his or her name and where he or she is from. Then the facilitator requests that people in the group volunteer information about that person from their interviews or from previous acquaintance.

Next the facilitator sits down, and the "interviewee" asks another person to come up and be interviewed. Thus the introductions proceed "round robin" style until everybody, including the facilitator, has been up in front of the group to be interviewed and to interview somebody else.

To the facilitator: This tool seems to work best in a group of 20 people or less. You can keep the pace going by allowing only a couple of minutes for each person to be in front of the group (timing can be shared by passing a watch around), or by asking that only a given number of people (e.g., 3-5 people) speak about each person.

---

* Sidney Simon, et al., *Values Clarification, a Handbook of Practical Strategies for Teachers and Students*, "Strategy #12, Public Interview." New York: Hart Publishing Co., Inc., 1972, pp. 139-157.

WHO CAN I MEET TODAY? (for young people aged about four to seven)

The facilitator interviews volunteers with a couple of light questions, such as "What's your whole name?" "What's your favorite kind of shoes?" "What's your favorite color?" and asks the children to suggest additional questions. (The volunteer sits on the facilitator's lap, or snuggles up close.)

Interviews in the Kitchen

Our family has been working on various ways to improve communication, and thereby to decrease conflict. We found that the interview process is a helpful tool for this.

A special time can be set aside to conduct an interview, or it can occur simultaneously with other activities. For instance, one evening our daughter Laura happily agreed that I interview her while I was preparing supper. Interviewing Laura helped me to understand her more fully as she described the saddest and happiest moments of her life. We were both enthusiastic about the interview, and she went on to interview me.

Before this set of interviews began Laura had had her heart set on french fries from the freezer for dinner. I'd already started making home fries—I assumed that a storm was in sight. But Laura was now perfectly willing to switch to home fries. I'm convinced that the warmth of the interviews made that transition peaceful.

—*Sue Taylor*

Interviews at Summer Camp

When I directed a summer camp, I began early in the summer to do interviews of children. Children volunteered, and two or three in one day would sit beside me in front of the group while I interviewed them.

Some children soon realized that they could use the interview process to talk about specific things they needed to discuss or wanted to share.

"Interview me on rocks, Chuck," one child asked. It turned out that he knew a tremendous amount about geology but had been reluctant to share it without some help.

"Interview me on divorce," another requested. Her parents had recently separated, and divorce was on her mind. By asking to be interviewed, she made it safe for other children with similar experiences to talk about their own situations.

Later in the summer we'd take long hikes. I remember a particularly long one when everybody was hot, hungry, tired, and irritable. As we were resting along the trail, one camper began spontaneously to interview another one.

"Do you remember a time when you felt like this?" ... "If you could be any place you wanted right now, where would you be and what would you be doing?"

Spirits began to lift. As we continued the hike, the campers paired up informally and interviewed each other. The interview process gave people a chance to pay attention to each other and to each other's feelings, and then to move on to other personal and involving topics.

—*Chuck Esser*

22

Sharing circles help to develop listening and speaking skills and to build trust within a group. Feelings, experiences, ideas and information can all be shared.

THEME CIRCLES

People are in a circle so that everybody can see each other. The facilitator introduces the theme for the day and explains or reviews the guidelines for sharing activities (p. 20). Then the facilitator gives each person a chance to share, by going around the circle or by asking people to speak when ready.

Sharing time ends with a game or a closing circle (p. 6), so that people's minds are back on the present and ready to focus on whatever happens next.

Sample sharing themes:
- A time when I felt really special...
- A Christmas that was disappointing...
- Something I wonder about...
- Something that happened to me when I was a baby...
- On the first day of my first school, I...

To the facilitator about timing: The time in sharing circles shouldn't be so long that participants become bored or quite fidgety. You can set the pace in several ways. You can be a model by being the first person to share on the topic. In any case, it is important that you take a turn, too. If you speak for one minute, chances are others will, too. If you speak longer, so will many others.

You can include in your review or explanation of the guidelines a statement of how much time you think it makes sense to spend in the sharing circle and about how much time each person will have to speak (e.g., "I think we'll take about twenty minutes to have our circle today. If everybody wants to speak, that means each of us gets to talk for one minute.")

If you decide that it's necessary to time the person talking so that everybody does get an equal turn, this timing can be a shared responsibility. Different people can be in charge of watching the clock and saying quietly, "Time," at the end of the allotted time for each speaker. Or a watch can be passed around the circle so each person gets a turn to time as well as to speak.

When people's attention is lagging and time seems to be dragging, it is often helpful to intersperse an "attention-out" activity (p. G-20).

Spontaneous Themes for Sharing Circles

I've found that themes for sharing will emerge spontaneously from my students. These themes are often more appropriate than any I could plan in advance.

For instance, one day at class meeting time, Judy shared that "Christina and Yvonne and I were playing outside yesterday and some big girls came and beat up Christina and she went to the hospital."

Yvonne and some other children who lived near her, who had already heard about the incident, shared their versions of the story. Several other children shared similar incidents they had experienced or knew about.

Although I hadn't planned on it, that meeting turned into a time for sharing "violent things that happen in our neighborhood." That's a pretty scary topic, but it triggered some of the best sharing that happened in my classroom.

—*Karen Zaur*

Participants are in a circle. The facilitator directs specific, varied questions to each participant. Some examples are:

"Sandy, do you remember a time when you laughed really hard? Tell us a little about it..."

"Derrick, do you remember a time when you made something that you really liked? What was it?"

To the facilitator: A random memory circle is helpful in a group with a limited attention span, since you as the facilitator are taking a more active role in setting the pace and in providing a variety of questions. You can take into consideration the needs and abilities of the group, and vary the questions from person to person to suit each one's needs. Encourage specific questions. At first, it may help to make a list of questions ahead of time.

One of the functions of random memory circles is to recognize a wider variety of human experiences in a short time. You may intersperse questions about unpleasant memories with questions about pleasant ones. However, good memories usually have some difficult aspects to them. Do not allow too much time to dwell on any particular difficulty or any one person's memory.

In order to maintain the pace and to hold the group's attention, this activity seems to work best when the facilitator moves fairly rapidly from one participant to the next.

Words to describe how we're feeling are powerful tools. They allow us the option of stating "what's going on" and releasing the tension that comes from holding the feelings inside. People who don't have a vocabulary to express feelings often are very frustrated and don't know what to do except keep the emotions bottled inside them, or release them in inappropriate ways—or even lash out physically.

Though having a feeling vocabulary is one step in being more in touch with our feelings, it's not a panacea. We'll still *have* the feelings to deal with, to try to release, sometimes to enjoy—and then to step past into responsible action. It is *not* okay to "dump" our feelings indiscriminately on other people, even with our new, impressive vocabulary! We must tell about our feelings thoughtfully and allow others to do the same.

All of the activities in this section help to build a feeling vocabulary. Class feeling books and student feeling books are special tools for this purpose.

FEELING BOOKS

A feeling book is a collection of a student's writing and drawing about his or her personal feelings. Older children enjoy writing about their feelings and illustrating the pages, or drawing without words. Younger children may draw and then dictate their descriptions of the pictures to the teacher to record onto the drawing. The pages are saved until there are enough to make a "book." Students like to make their own covers and bind the pages together.

Note: These "books" may be combined with the pages of the "I'm Great" book for a longer collection by and about the student. (p. 9).

Instead of each student having a feeling book for herself or himself, a class may decide it wants to combine all the writings and/or drawings about one emotion into a book for the whole class (e.g., "The Sad Book," "The Happy Book"). Such a book can be available in the classroom for individuals to read to help recognize how they and others feel; it can be used for reading aloud as a group and for further discussion about feelings; and it can be kept as a durable record of the class at a particular time during the school year.

Students write and/or draw descriptions of their feelings (see procedure for feeling books). After they have shared their descriptions with each other, the pages are bound into a notebook, which is placed where everybody can read it.

Materials: same as for a feeling book. A sturdy two or three-ring notebook is helpful.

Note: An individual student may not wish to have his or her writing or drawing made public in a class book. That wish, of course, should always be respected.

Affirming the "Physically Expressive"

Children most frequently punished in school are those who physically hurt other children during an argument. While I was teaching at the Children's School, I became increasingly aware of how unfair this often is. When a child would come to me to complain of being hit or scratched, I would of course be concerned and unhappy with the child who had done the hurting. On second look, however, I often noticed that the child who had been hurt physically had done a lot of hurting too—verbally. Verbally skilled children are able to manipulate less verbal children into actions that get them into trouble. Since we strongly encourage children to use their voices instead of their hands, the verbal child may get tacit approval for this manipulation while the physically expressive child gets punished. How can we give more loving approval to the physically expressive child?

—*Karen Zaur*

Ditto Books

The fifth and sixth grade students I work with aren't used to working together or to listening to each other. But they love to make dittos, and they get excited about reading what they've written when it's printed out on a ditto sheet. So we've turned ditto making into a cooperative venture.

When a child has completed a story which she or he really likes, I encourage him or her to make a "book." This includes a neat copy, usually accompanying illustrations, a title page and a cover. Some children read these aloud to a group or to the class. Some simply put the book on a special shelf. Students often pick up these books to read, and they usually tell the author how much they like them. "Your dragon picture was great."

We've also created "books" by making a collection. Each person who wants to be an author of the book does a short story, usually with illustrations, on a page-sized ditto. These are run off, then collated by every child who wants a book, and stapled together. The students are hugely congratulatory to each other on their stories. Everyone in class usually wants one of these books, whether or not she or he has a story in it.

I'm planning to have the class write its own notebook for science by asking each student to take responsibility for a certain area, e.g., the digestive system, and to do a dittoed worksheet for others on it, unlabelled, uncolored. Each student will explain his or her worksheet in class so the others can label and color it in. All these sheets will be put together into a workbook on the whole body. Each student will have a workbook to work with and to refer to later in the year, when we compare other vertebrates to ourselves.

Making dittos can be a strong sharing and affirmation activity in itself. Even though they find it difficult to listen to individual or group reports, everybody appreciates each other's ditto pages. Students congratulate each other on their work and are proud of themselves.

—*Sioux Baldwin*

Writing Every Day

Early in the school year, my sixth grade class and I brainstormed a list of feelings. One of the students copied the list from the blackboard, and we kept it on my desk. Every morning before the students arrived, I chose three or four feelings to put on the board. ("Happiness is..." "I feel annoyed when..." "Loneliness is...")

Each day began with everybody—including myself—completing the sentences or writing about anything else that seemed more important and "on top." I read the papers (without the author's name) out loud, except for those that had "Please don't read" at the top—a signal that they were too personal to be read before the class. (The students also kept journals, which I *never* read. There they could write things that they didn't want *anyone* to read.)

The time spent reading the papers aloud was special for us, and provided a good variation on a sharing circle. Later that year, we compiled our writings to make an illustrated, dittoed book for the whole school—an affirming enterprise for sixth graders who had thought in September that they "hated to write."
— *Stephanie Judson*

A Visit to Grandparents

When my youngest daughter Ingrid was four years old, our family all flew to Norway to visit my parents and relatives. Of course, there were inevitable intergenerational tensions. I was concerned that the children "behave" for their grandparents —my mother and father. Yet I've realized that as such, I set up standards of behavior for the children which were different from those at home in Philadelphia.

Ingrid pointed this out beautifully. One day of our visit, she began to cry over her disappointment about the day's plans. In Philadelphia, we encourage the children to cry when they need to. But that day, with my parents, I immediately tried to hush her up.

Ingrid sat up with surprise.

"I'm letting my feelings out," she replied clearly and indignantly, and she returned to finish with her tears.
— *Berit Lakey*

Puppets and Feelings

Young children play with puppets in much the same way that they play with dolls. They use puppets to experiment with different roles and feelings and to try out different ways of being together.

Large, readily available supplies of sock puppets in the classroom and at home provide opportunities to act experiences and feelings through play.

Books which remind children of their own experiences can be helpful in leading to puppet play. *The Quarreling Book* (p. 108) and *Minoo's Family* (p. 105) are two good examples. After hearing such stories, children can be encouraged to act them out, using sock puppets or simply their own bodies.

A longer description of the use of puppets appears in the Conflict Resolution section, pp. 41.

"I Wish I Were Sick"

"I wish I were sick. Would you take my temperature, Mom?"

I asked my eight-year-old son what was troubling him. Peter groaned, "I HATE newspaper at school. You have only 15 minutes to write your story and you're not allowed to write it ahead of time. I can't do it."

Some of my own past school experiences suddenly became painfully alive, deadening my ability to listen. I wanted to protect Peter. Unable to stop myself, I started saying things like, "Did you talk to the newspaper teacher?...Maybe if you tell your regular teacher she can do something."

"It won't do any good." Peter wasn't ready to hear my solutions for his problem.

Hal, my husband, began reflecting back Peter's feelings to him. "You wish you didn't have to go to school."

"Yes!" was the close-to-tears reply.

"It seems too hard to have to write that story," Hal continued.

"Mm-hmm."

At breakfast the next morning, Peter was still unhappy. Now I found that I could listen. "You feel as if there is nothing you can do about newspaper time....It really is frustrating to have only 15 minutes to write your story." Definite affirmative responses followed. Peter grudgingly left for school.

When I arrived to take him home after school, Peter was enthusiastically playing with friends. I initiated, "How did newspaper go?"

"Fine! I wrote two stories in 15 minutes."

Peter's stories have continued to come with ease. All we did was listen, reflect back, and listen some more.

—Sue Taylor

Children's Literature

Many children's books about feelings are beautifully and sensitively written. A list of such books which we've found particularly effective is included in the Books section, pp. 105-108.

"Just Like Us"

I remember the first time my co-teacher Jessica read *Minoo's Family* (see p. 105) to the class. Sharon and Richard kept interrupting to say, "That's just like what happened to us." And it was.

Sharon and Richard had moved to our school neighborhood with their mother about a year before. They remembered feeling afraid when they heard their parents' angry voices, just like Minoo. It had made them feel sad and cry, just like Minoo. And they remembered finding out for sure that their parents had decided not to live together any more, just like Minoo's. Just like Minoo, they and Mommy have new friends, but they continue to miss Daddy, whom they visit on weekends.

By the end of the story, Richard and Sharon had moved to be as close to Jessica as possible. The story sparked lots of sharing from other children and adults, too. But the story seemed to belong to Sharon and Richard in a special way.

The next time I saw their mother, I told her about the book. We loaned her the school copy and encouragingly told her where she might buy one.

—Karen Zaur

Without Any Words

Neither of my parents are given to open demonstrations of feelings. My father, a very sensitive man, seems duty-bound to keep up a "strong" appearance in times of stress. This internalizing of his feelings has caused him several major heart attacks, yet no amount of advice has freed him to let his feelings out.

One afternoon my father and I were alone talking matter-of-factly about a family crisis. It was obvious that the solution to the problem did not lie in our hands. Daddy quietly moved away from me and stood staring out the window; the anguish on his face showed clearly that he felt he had failed. On an impulse I crossed the room and gave him a long silent hug—saying without words that I knew that he had done his very best—and for a few miraculous moments he cried.

—An intuitive daughter

Feelings, experiences, and information are all elements that people can share with each other. In doing so, we retain and regain our humanness. Structured sharing activities can help us to do this. They can also help us to reach for, but cannot and should not replace, precious moments of spontaneous sharing.

Conflict Resolution

Conflict and Choice

We Have a Choice

Most of us have little background in dealing successfully with conflict. Some of us were sheltered from it as children, though we had upsetting experiences when conflict did erupt. Others had conflict heaped on us when we were too young to feel as if we could take control of the situation. Either way, we connect conflict with fearful or angry responses and avoid it or react belligerently. And either way, we have not had much opportunity to experience or to think about the various approaches to dealing with conflict, nor do we have much confidence that it's possible to resolve it.

Meanwhile, it continues to be an everyday part of our lives, whether we let it lie buried beneath the surface, where it often smolders and from which it sometimes erupts; or whether we recognize and acknowledge it, which is the first step toward being able to resolve it nonviolently. We have a choice!

Choosing to Act

Any change in any situation starts with at least one person taking a concrete step. This is true for a conflict situation: change will occur when one or more people begin to act. Therefore, whenever we recognize and acknowledge conflict, we've also recognized an opportunity to change the situation by taking some action. It's true that taking that step

may require a lot of thinking and energy. Taking that action may require overcoming, or setting aside, a lot of timidity. But it's worth it!

Taking a concrete step also requires contradicting the idea that a situation is hopeless and that we're helpless in solving it. That hopeless/helpless feeling derives partly from our fixed, set ways of thinking. "It's always been that way.... There's no other way to go about it...we *tried* that already."

We're not helpless, and it's not hopeless. Any human activity which jostles our minds can provide new, fresh ways of thinking about a problem and can contradict our belief that it's hopeless.

Laying the Groundwork

This section includes several ways to help people think about, explore, and resolve conflict. It is, of course, important to lay the groundwork for conflict resolution by establishing a spirit of affirmation, sharing, and supportive community. If this is done, conflict will be reduced, and can become an enjoyable challenge! Therefore, the other parts of this manual concentrate on areas which lay the groundwork.

29

Conflict About Rules and Discipline

Rules and discipline are two frequent areas of
conflict. Here is some thinking about each area.

RULES

Rules are, at best, thoughtful guidelines for
behavior. Of course, they're important! Children
expect them from parents and teachers. Everybody
seeks out leaders whom they trust to articulate and
enforce thoughtful guidelines.

However, the term "rules" sometimes connotes
rigid restrictions and resistance. So we've found that
"policy" is a more useful word. In our work with
nonviolence and children we've assumed that:

1) Good policy helps people to interact with
   each other and with their environment with
   love, care, and safety.

2) Everybody basically wants to interact this
   way, even though hurts and feelings sometimes get in the way of actually doing it.

Good policy is made by thinking about the
situation at hand and asking the question, "What
rules do we need here to help everybody involved
interact lovingly, caringly, and safely with each other
and with the environment?" Once it is formulated,
the leader presents the policy firmly, factually, and
unaccusingly to the people involved—and then listens
to the response. If some part of the policy doesn't
make sense, somebody is likely to recognize that it
doesn't, and say so.

For instance, at the beginning of the school year,
a kindergarten teacher was reviewing with his class
the school rules that students had to pair up, hold
hands, and walk the entire way to the playground
two blocks from the school. Many students
grumbled. The teacher responded that the rule was

made for their safety, so that students wouldn't be
run over when they crossed the street. More
grumbling, though quieter, ensued. Then a child
stated clearly, "We want to run when it's safe." The
students and teacher talked some more. They defined
where it was safe to run and where it wasn't safe. The
teacher changed policy for his class accordingly.

DISCIPLINE

Sometimes children (and adults!) do not agree with policy that *does* make sense. Their own hurts and feelings get in the way of their acting lovingly, caringly, and safely with others and with their environment. When this happens they need to release their feelings and get rid of their hurts. However, it is *never* appropriate for them to act out or hurt themselves or others when they have these feelings; it is appropriate for the person in charge to interrupt such behavior. Interrupting the behavior, stating the policy firmly, and encouraging feelings to be released when possible is what we call *discipline*.

It's important to look for the difference between actually releasing feelings and "getting them out of the system," and *acting* in a destructive way that's determined by feelings. We can often trust our own intuitions and common sense to see the difference. A good guideline is to look for actual release of feelings —tears, shaking, laughter, etc. If a child is crying, he or she is not merely *playing* for attention, as we've been encouraged to assume. The crying is a signal that the child *needs* attention, and will likely use it well to get the hurt out.

If a child is whining or showing some disruptive behavior, (needling, name-calling, putting down, yelling,) or if a child is retreating, being unusually quiet and sluggish, then it's time to interrupt, or stop the behavior. If possible, it's appropriate to encourage the child to release the feelings.

"...Going to Kill..."

Five-year-old Phillip came in from the playground and was stamping around, head down. He knocked down somebody's carefully-built block tower, muttering under his breath, "I am really going to kill Jerome."

I put my arms around Phillip and asked him what was happening. He told me more about how he was going to kill Jerome. I asked about Jerome; Phillip replied that Jerome had hit him on the playground. I listened and encouraged him to pretend that I was Jerome, and to show me how he was going to kill me. (I knew that Phillip would not actually be able to hurt me, which I wouldn't have allowed him to do anyway. And I kept holding onto him.)

He punched me once. Then he started to cry, telling me how much he missed his Daddy. After crying for a short time, he was ready to participate in our program for the day, and he enjoyed it.

—*Chuck Esser*

Thoughts About Anger

Editor's Note: *Many people ask us about anger. Anger is often associated with conflict. Therefore, before going on to conflict resolution activities and approaches, we offer our thinking about anger.*

We've all experienced anger. We've felt it rise up in ourselves and we've seen it in other people. Like other natural human emotions, it can be choked down and suppressed or it can be effectively, and undestructively, released. Since expressions of anger are scary, people often carry their anger around with them, bottling it up inside for fear that it might erupt destructively. However, bottling it up doesn't work. The anger is still visible to others in one form or another, but difficult to deal with openly, since it's "below the surface."

Rather than holding it in, people can get anger out of their systems by "storming," "raging," or having a "temper tantrum." This kind of release is not to be confused with breaking things, physically hurting people or putting them down. Genuine storming, raging, and temper tantrums need not hurt anybody.

The most effective way to help somebody release anger in this way is to listen attentively, be affirming and loving, and encourage the anger to come. When the storm is over, the person will be in a much better position to deal with the issues at hand.

Real anger is usually rooted in righteous indignation about injustice. We may experience anger from injustice which happens to us directly, or which happens around us. A situation from the present may remind us of an unjust situation from the past, when we didn't get a chance to show our anger or to correct the situation. At such times, that past anger may easily come to the surface.

Whether the injustice is from the past or the present, it has originated outside ourselves. Therefore, we need not apologize for our anger, nor criticize others for theirs. Of course, there may be situations in which it's not appropriate to storm or rage, no matter how angry we feel. And again, it's never appropriate to be destructive of others when we are angry, nor should we allow children or other adults to do so.

When Children Are Angry

Children often have an easier time than adults in releasing anger, because they've had fewer years to practice bottling it up. However, they still usually need help and encouragement to release it.

When an adult interrupts a child's (or another adult's!) destructive behavior, and encourages the child to release anger, the child will probably start to storm or rage, i.e. to yell, cry, and struggle physically. Of course, the child is likely to direct anger at the adult, whether or not the adult was the originator of the injustice. So the adult should expect this barrage, be physically and verbally affirming, and encourage the child to keep right on raging. When the raging is over, they will be friends again.

Since anger seems scary, the adult may feel hurt or scared about being stormed at. He or she should deal with these feelings later, with another adult who understands the feelings and agrees to listen.

Storming and raging are natural processes to release anger. Once it is released, people are often more easily able to think clearly about correcting the unjust situation which caused the anger in the first place.

32

Problem-Solving Approaches

The rest of this section contains a variety of approaches to solving problems. First, Karen Zaur writes of her experience in the classroom. Karen taught kindergarten, first, and second grades for several years before joining the Nonviolence and Children Collective. Other collective members also contribute to these pages through anecdotes about their own experiences.

Next, parents and other teachers follow with "More Approaches to Solving Problems" (p.39). Finally, the "Goal-Wish Problem-Solving" method is outlined (p.44), followed by anecdotes of two different experiences using adaptations of this method.

The activities and approaches in this section are intended to increase people's ability to think in conflict situations. Some of them jiggle our minds and stir our imaginations. Others provide listening so that a person is freer to think about the problem. None of these activities will work well if we rely on them alone instead of on our own thinking abilities. Each activity is to help us think, not to do our thinking for us.

A Classroom Teacher's Experience

by Karen Zaur

Editor's Note: *These approaches in problem-solving, which Karen Zaur has contributed from her years in teaching, seem equally applicable to situations at home and other contexts outside the classroom.*

At some point in my teaching experience I realized that children who came to me with problems didn't necessarily expect me to solve them. What a relief! In fact, finding solutions often seemed to be a focus imposed by adults. That realization encouraged me to think about ways I might help children be in charge of their own problems and ways I could better take charge of my own. Here are some of the ways I've considered and tried.

Listening

There are countless themes around which children complain, from something which someone else has done to them to a bump or a scratch they have received. I have learned to listen carefully to the whole story and then ask simply, "Did he stop it?" or "Are you okay now?" The answer was often *yes*, and the child, having had a chance to tell the story, returned to the activities at hand.

Learning Useful Phrases

My co-teacher Jessica Agre and I encouraged children to tell the person who was bothering them, "Stop it! I don't like that." When it was necessary, we not only suggested what children say, but also stood by them while they said it. Standing by meant holding both children, reminding the speaker to use a loud voice, and asking the listener if he or she had heard and understood what was being said.

When Jessica or I had a chance to tell another person in the classroom "Stop that! I don't like it!" we were also modelling the use of the phrases. Implicitly, we were conveying "This is something we grownups do, too." Modelling such phrases is a way of giving children another tool for handling *their* problems. Children are more likely to add this tool to their repertoire when they hear it used by others.

Providing Safety

We hoped to give the children a sense that they could protect themselves from being hurt, verbally or physically. At the Children's School the ground rule for dealing with someone who is bugging you is, "First say, 'Stop it!' Say it in a loud voice, and if that doesn't help, come and tell a teacher." As teachers, we were also available for protection.

When children were physically hurting each other or otherwise being excessively nasty, a teacher would go with them to a quiet place. We provided safety by holding one or both of them or sometimes by just being there as they got the feelings out and worked the problem through.

Getting It Settled Without a Teacher

Often children who have been fighting with each other will present two very different versions of what happened. It became our policy at those times to ask the children involved to go to a quiet place in the building which was free from distraction until they settled the problem themselves and were "ready to come back."

We didn't necessarily expect to hear the settlement, but we did expect children who returned to the room to be able to act civilly toward each other. For me, the hardest thing about this was realizing that I didn't need to know exactly what had happened.

"You're a Liar!"

One day I overheard two children whom Jessica had asked to settle a fight they had been having during the class meeting. She had simply told them to leave and to come back when they were ready.

At first there were a lot of accusations on both sides: "You're a liar." "No, YOU are a liar." "It's not my fault." "Yes, it is! It's your fault and you're a liar."

After several minutes the accusations became less frequent and I heard one of the children hesitantly say, "We-e-l-l, it *was* a 'little bit' my fault." Quiet, and then a similar comment from the other child. "Well, it was a little my fault, too, I guess." They agreed that they were ready to go back to the meeting.

One of them called out to Jessica, "Can we come back?" She asked, "Are you ready?" They answered, "Yes." And back they went.

—Karen Zaur

Piano Practice

I had just gotten home from work and was feeling tired, headachey, and cranky about having to struggle with dinner. Kurt, 9, and Gregg, 8, anxious to get outside to play, were arguing over who would do his half hour of piano practice first. Angrily, I demanded that they take turns; one of them reading for half an hour while the other one played piano. Neither could go out until both had practiced. "That's not fair, we'll never get out of here!" Kurt pouted.

Suddenly I remembered some of Karen Zaur's notes on problem-solving that I had read at work that day. "Talk straight"... "Let the children solve their own problems." Just the advice I needed.

"I am feeling miserable," I said calmly, "and I don't want to argue with you. I am going into the kitchen to try to get my work done. You can both go out when you have solved your problem with the piano practice."

After a few very quiet minutes I heard music from the living room. Half an hour later both boys marched matter-of-factly through the kitchen with their coats on. "Don't worry, Mom," Kurt announced. "We figured out a great system. One of us plays for fifteen minutes while the other one studies his music theory, and then we switch. This way we both get done in one half hour!"

—Lois Dorn

Acting as a Third Party

Sometimes it seemed appropriate for a teacher to be a neutral person in order to begin the process of "dispute settlement." In these cases, Jessica or I listened to both sides first, then asked the children to work it out by themselves.

"You'll Have to Figure It Out"

One day when I was in Karen's classroom, Daryll and Mitch stormed in, fresh from fighting with each other on the playground. They both began talking to Jessica at once. Jessica sat down between the two boys and said that she wanted to hear what had happened—from each of them. She asked Mitch to go first, and then Daryll.

After Jessica had listened carefully to both boys, she said, "You each have a different story about what happened on the playground, and I wasn't there to see it. So I don't know what the answer is. You'll have to go outside the room and talk about it together and figure out what to do. As soon as you figure it out, come and tell me what you've decided."

Daryll and Mitch looked at each other dubiously, then at Jessica. It was evident that she meant it—she wasn't going to give them an answer, and she did believe that they could work it out together.

"C'mon, Mitch," Daryll said, standing up. They went out onto the steps. Fifteen minutes later, they reappeared. "It's okay. We're friends, Jessica," they assured her. "Do you want to tell me what you figured out?" she asked. "That's what we figured out," they replied.

—*Ellen Forsythe*

Children as Third Parties

I spent a lot of time last year with my fifth grade class being a third party negotiator or mediator between various warring individuals. "You talk first, and tell me what happened, and then he'll get a chance," I'd explain to one party. "You be quiet, and then you'll get a turn as soon as he's done," I'd say to the other. I had to be *very* firm; they were usually *very* angry at the beginning of the process.

Towards the end of the school year, some students themselves started to act as third party negotiators for their classmates. This was a good sign. I knew that I had *really* been effective though, when the music teacher came up to me this year.

"Two of your students from last year were in a tremendous fight when they arrived at music class today," she recounted. "They came up to me and asked if they could leave the room with a third person to mediate. They told me they knew how to do that from fifth grade. Amazing! Of course I said yes."

—*Keith Miller*

36

Talking Straight

I think of "talking straight" as a way of levelling with a person, of saying, "Look, this is what I see you doing," and of involving the person in solving the problem.

At staffings, (see p.84) I often suggest that teachers try the "talking straight" approach. For example, Nancy's teacher was especially concerned about her "tuning out" at group times. The staffing group offered Nancy's teacher a number of fine recommendations: provide more art materials (Nancy's special interest), foster possible friendships at school through art projects and at home by contacting parents, actively pay attention to her, create more classroom jobs for which she might like to be responsible, and so forth.

I added, "Be straight with Nancy about what you see happening at group time and what your expectations are. Let her know that you really want her to be part of the group. Involve Nancy in dealing with the problem." For example, Nancy might have a special friend she'd like to sit near at group time. Perhaps nothing at group time has interested her. How could the teacher know this without talking with Nancy? It's too easy—actually too hard—for this to be a problem the teachers will tackle alone.

Talking Straight with Whining

Karen's discussion about "talking straight" reminds me of my own experience. In my four and five year old class, Andrea came to whine and hang onto me every few minutes. Previously, I had tried showing her with my face how this complaining looked. She had laughed a lot at this, but she hadn't stopped whining and hanging on. So I said, firmly, "Now you stop that right now." She did, and went brightly back to working independently.

—*Chuck Esser*

On Rotten Moods

There were times when, for any number of reasons, I wasn't able to implement a single one of the problem-solving techniques above. Sometimes I would announce, "I don't want to hear about it!" Sometimes I would be less polite than that and just scream at someone.

That usually made me feel like an ogre. I learned, however, that the children were open to accepting that sometimes I felt "very grouchy." Occasionally, at meeting time, I would tell the class that I was tired, headachey, or feeling generally rotten and didn't want to be bothered a lot. They understood what I meant. Once a child told me, "My mother says that sometimes." I remember overhearing comments like, "Let's not tell Karen; she isn't in a very good mood."

It is equally important to recognize that children feel very grouchy sometimes, too. Some options are extra attention for the child, a quiet place for getting away from it all, a day off from some work or job in the classroom, a phone call home, and some thought about what might need changing in the classroom.

A Broad View of Classroom Problems

As I was running a workshop for teachers, it occurred to me that the annoying "little" problems which come up time and time again in the classroom actually boil down to a few basic themes. I'm talking about problems such as, "You never pick me...." "She took my puzzle...." "Do I have to come to the meeting?"

As I perceive it, the themes represented here and in countless other upsets involve:

- trying to get enough attention
- questions of property, particularly sharing
- what I call "making space," or feeling free to move in and out of social interactions.

When I substituted the term "needs" for "themes," I realized that school often is not set up to meet those needs. Moreover, adults have those needs, too. Most adults I know would cringe at the thought of "having" to interact with thirty or so peers from 9 a.m. to 3 p.m. Monday through Friday. Yet that is exactly what school is all about.

I wonder a lot about what we can do as teachers and as human beings to meet those needs. First, and perhaps most important, we can recognize the needs. This can help to prevent us from reacting in a blaming and annoyed way when, for example, a particular child can't find his or her jacket at 3:00 p.m.

We must continue to respect the feelings and information which children share with us, and to give, when possible, the attention they request. We must be aware that it is often difficult to share property. I personally do not think that children under five or so should be told that they "have to" share their belongings. Making time and space for doing things alone as well as for small and large group activities respects children's "space" needs. That means that time and space for individuals should be an everyday occurrence, not just a way to deal with a child having a "bad day."

Parents, teachers, and concerned citizens can work together as political advocates for children. We can lobby, pressure, and organize for a smaller teacher/student ratio which would provide more attention for children. We can demand adequate classroom supplies. We can work towards school architecture which provides the kinds of individual space which we all deserve.

These kinds of changes do not necessarily require more funds. For example, the 1970 cost per pupil for the Children's School facility (demolition of one house, and renovation of one house) was less than half the per pupil cost to build new elementary schools in Philadelphia in the same year.*

Children's problems/children's needs/human problems/human needs—they are all so related. We can act with that in mind.

Laying the Groundwork for Problem-Solving with Parents

When I was student teaching, I noticed from the beginning how often my cooperating teacher, Arlene Ross, made opportunities to connect with parents. She would call them to relay bits of official school information, to inquire about children who had missed a few days of school, and even to offer to pick up something at the store for parents who were home with a sick child or who weren't feeling well themselves. These phone calls allowed her to establish relationships between herself and a parent before a time came when they had to sit down to talk about hard things, difficulties with the child.

In my own teaching, I worked on those informal relationships with parents. Sometimes I had to stretch to find openings to make contact. I'd make a list of parents I especially wanted to talk with and then make phone calls to remind them about the class trip, school photographs, or whatever, instead of sending notes home.

Of course I wasn't able to establish close relationships with all the parents. But at least they connected a voice with my name. They knew that I was concerned about the child, and they didn't immediately associate me with trouble.

But I did develop several lasting personal friendships with the parents of the children whom I taught. And this is not a small benefit!

* Source of figures: Philadelphia Board of Education, cited in *A Proposal for Small Elementary Schools Modelled after the Mantua-Powelton Children's School*, prepared by Mantua-Powelton Co-operative Educational Fund.

More Approaches to Solving Problems

by other teachers and parents

Editor's Note: *We continue this section with more approaches to solving problems and more examples, contributed by a variety of people.*

Breaking Tension with Physical Activity

Physical activity can help to break the tension which often builds up when a large number of children are in a limited space. Cooperative games are very helpful for this. Teachers who are not afraid of seeming silly can try almost anything, as Sandy Branam indicates.

In a Montessori Classroom

by Sandy Branam

Sometimes a good deal of tension builds in my classroom of 2½ to 6 year olds, due to a large number of young children together in a small space, or a rainy day, or whatever. I returned from my first Nonviolence and Children Workshop full of enthusiasm and ideas on how to break this tension when it built.

First I tried acting like an unidentifiable animal making sort of huffing and woofing sounds and asking the children to join in. They thought I was out of my skull, but it did break the tension.

Then I tried shaking hands. But as some had their hands in water, and others in paint, some were upset by this.

Finally I tried clapping. They caught on instantly. Now with just one clap, they are ready for the rhythm to be set. Sometimes I hear, "Yeah, let's clap," as grins spread across their delighted faces.

They love it when someone suddenly breaks into a joyous song. A favorite of mine is "Oh, What a Beautiful Morning!" but a very quiet song is better if they are being rowdy.

Using Children's Books

Children's books can provide examples of people resolving their conflicts creatively and nonviolently. A list of such books which we've found to be particularly effective is included in the Books section (pp. 104-105).

Such books can also provide information which children can use to solve their own problems. Chuck Esser gives an example from his class of four to five year olds.

"Girls Not Allowed"

by Chuck Esser

There was a lot of talk in my class about how girls can't play on the jungle gym, and so forth. I had told the girls and boys that the things in the classroom were for everyone to use, that girls were as strong as boys. Then I decided to read to the class some books with girls as strong stars. I read *The Magic Hat* and *Mommies at Work* (pp. 104 and 109). The next day I heard one of the boys saying, "They can *too* play here. You know they can be sailors just like in *Mommies at Work*."

Humor

Humor is an element which will jiggle our minds out of a set way of approaching a problem into new ways of thinking. Therefore, humor will often open the way for the resolution of conflict. This doesn't mean making fun of somebody, of course. The accompanying anecdotes by Sue Taylor and Ann Bauer illustrate the concept.

"Banana in the Bathtub!"

My daughter Kate (age 3½) and I were boxed into a recurring struggle. Kate would begin by asking for something which I couldn't or wouldn't give, and I would begin by feeling ungenerous and guilty about my lack of generosity. From there we would escalate. Often she ended with a tantrum, and I ended feeling awful.

Once when this had already started, I put her in the bathtub to give myself (and her) some space. **She demanded a banana!** I was so outraged that I couldn't see the humor in her demand. What was actually ridiculous I perceived as most unreasonable.

It was only when I was recounting the scene to a friend, who laughed heartily, that I could see the humor in it.

A week or so later, when I was putting Kate to bed, we talked about it and *she* laughed. I told her that in the future, whenever she made a demand which I felt was aimed at "getting" me, I was going to call it a "Banana in the Bathtub."

The next time she made a demand like that, I forgot and got mad. But the time after that, I remembered. I was angry, but I just said, out loud to myself, "Banana, banana, banana," for about two minutes. Meanwhile, she was waiting for her doll—which we'd left at home. Then I said, "Kate, that's a 'Banana in the Bathtub.'" She dropped the subject, and so did I. The whole escalator collapsed.

Since then, she hasn't done that number very many times. "Banana in the Bathtub" is as good a giggle-getter as tickling. The last time I accused her of demanding a "Banana in the Bathtub," she said, thoughtfully and reasonably, without any tears or demands, "I don't think it is."

Now we have a meaningful label which we can use to talk about something that used to steamroll us.

—Ann Bauer

"The Element of Surprise"

One memorable morning during a brawl involving three of our children, I applied some creativity I had learned from the parent support group. The night before, we had talked about the element of surprise as one aspect of conflict resolution. Stephanie had pointed out that surprising the person involved in destructive behavior may interrupt the violence. So, feeling calm from a good night's sleep, I lifted the lid of the laundry hamper, put my ear to it, and exclaimed, "What did you say? No kidding!" There was astonished silence, followed by a roar of laughter. That little distraction changed the climate so completely that problem-solving was able to follow.

—Sue Taylor
Reprinted from Fellowship, *October, 1975*

A Pencil Fight

A while back, I was working in a first- and second-grade classroom at a table with three children. Two of them, Stella and Michael, began to fight over a pencil.

"It's my pencil!" "No, it's not, it's mine!"

I suspected that the pencil wasn't the real problem but rather that they were bored and restless.

"Hold it!" I said. "Looks to me like you're not really fighting over a pencil. And I know for a fact that you're friends. Why don't you tell me something you like about each other?"

Stella and Michael balked at first, but with encouragement they managed to affirm each other. They resolved the pencil question with generosity, Stella proceeding to do a drawing with Michael's name and giving it to him.

—*Ellen Deacon*

Thoughts to the Collective

I think that this (the pencil fight) is a good example of using affirmation to turn a negative situation around. And it also brings up two issues for me that we need to think about.

First, I bet that Ellen is right that Stella and Michael were bored and restless, that the pencil wasn't the problem. And if Ellen is right, then how do we go a step further to encourage change in the school structure so that restlessness and boredom aren't there to deal with? Certainly Ellen did the right thing given the problem. But the situation itself needs to be changed.

Second, I think that we need to be clear with ourselves that we should not deny negative feelings if they *are* there. Affirmation must not be equated with "Pollyannaism." Negative feelings must be recognized and dealt with.

Finally, we need to be clear that we should not interpret others' feelings for them.

—*Stephanie Judson*

Puppetry and Conflict

Role-playing is a well-known method of exploring conflict, trying out different solutions, and gaining insights. We have found that puppets are an exciting medium for role-playing. Puppets provide enough of a sense of theater and make-believe for children to feel safe to act out conflicts. Therefore, a large part of this section is devoted to puppetry as a means for exploring conflict. Again, the examples here come mainly from the classroom. They can be adapted to home and other contexts.

Puppet Skits in the Classroom

One way to use puppets to explore conflict is for the teacher to present a "real-life" problem in skit form to the students.* For instance, the teacher starts an argument between the two sock puppets he or she is wearing.

"You took my book."

"What do you mean? It's MY book."

With common sense and a little imagination, skits such as this can be generated on the spot. The skit builds to a point where a decision must be made. At this point, the puppet turns to the audience and says, "What should I do?" Members of the audience must decide the possible courses of action.

There are several possibilities for working together on the problem the puppets have presented. Here are three:

1) The group can be divided into threes or fours to discuss the problem.

2) The participants can turn to the persons next to them to discuss the problem.

3) The entire group can work together in a brainstorming fashion. The following questions are useful for discussion:
   - "What is the problem?"
   - "Exactly what happened?"
   - "How did ＿＿ feel? How did ＿＿ feel?"

* The account of work in the Children's School also contains a description of this approach.

41

After these questions are discussed, the group can take a few moments to create solutions to the problem. When everyone has thought of a solution, the solutions are acted out for the group one by one, using puppets.

After each solution is presented, the teacher asks the entire group, "Do you think that this solution would work?" (Or, after all the solutions have been presented, the facilitator asks, "Which ones would work?") This is an important question to ask. Often one of the solutions will be physically violent or otherwise destructive. By being asked consistently, "Would that work?" people are encouraged to think about it more. This is preferable to "putting down" the solution or declaring it unacceptable. If children know that they won't be "put down," they will feel safe to work off frustration, anger, or other pent-up feelings by acting out rather violent solutions with puppets.

Using puppetry this way encourages people to think about a problem while they are not in the heat of the argument and also provides an opportunity for people to hear a variety of responses to conflict. Children often begin to suggest conflicts from their own lives as topics for skits.

A Puppetry Session

In a session with second graders, Sally, age seven, described an ongoing argument with her sister, complaining that when her younger sister played with Sally's games she broke and lost pieces of them.

Using sock puppets, Sally and a friend who volunteered as younger sister acted out the skit for the group. I asked them to stop at the point when the toys were being broken. Her classmates volunteered ideas, taking turns acting the part of her younger sister, while Sally continued to play herself, still using a puppet.

Sally had already considered most of the ideas which her classmates suggested. However, the session offered her a chance to think more about the problem. Then she herself thought of still another solution: the games could stay in her room while her sister played with them. A few days later, Sally reported that her own solution was working.

Note: It might also have been helpful for Sally to act the role of her sister in order to understand her sister's position better.

—*Ellen Forsythe*

Two Puppet Skits for Exploring Conflict

The Clique

Characters:

Amanda (in the clique, but she likes Nina, too)
Nina (the outsider, new in this school this year)
Susan (the leader of the clique)
Betsy (another clique member)

Nina and Amanda talk after school on a Friday. Nina asks Amanda to come over and spend the night, talks of her loneliness, says that Amanda is her only friend, mentions how mean the girls in the clique have been to her.

Amanda accepts the invitation, says she has to meet Susan and Betsy first and will come over to Nina's later. Nina leaves. Susan and Betsy enter, talking about the school day. Susan tells them she's planning a slumber party for that night. They talk about who's invited (the others in the clique). Amanda says Nina has invited her, suggests they both come. Susan and Betsy snicker about Nina, say some mean things, and then tell Amanda that she has to make a choice, "Either Nina or us!" Cut, and open for discussion.

TV Fight

Louise, the older one, is playing with blocks al. over the TV-playroom area. She leaves for a few minutes, and in walks Joey, who turns on the TV and begins watching a favorite show, oblivious to the mess of blocks around him. Louise comes back in and indignantly states that she had the room first and will he please shut off the TV. He says he was in the room first and no, he will not turn off the TV. She insists, he resists. She turns off the TV. He turns it on again. This happens several times and then, out of sheer frustration, she hits him. He cries and runs out of the room, threatening to tell Mom. What happens next? How could this have been avoided?

Using Puppets with Preschoolers

by Kathy Allen

In the Red Wagon Day Care Center, a conflict occurs almost daily with "clean-up." To present the problem another teacher and I used four puppets, three serving as children and one as a grownup. All played with lots of toys on the stage—blocks, cars, dolls, mattress (a small pillow), books, paint brushes, etc. Then the grownup said, "Five more minutes till clean-up time." The three puppets grumbled. When clean-up time arrived, all the children puppets started giving excuses why they couldn't clean up. "I'm too tired..." "I feel sick..." "My legs hurt...." "I didn't play with that!..." "I have to go to the bathroom...." "I just started this puzzle, and it will take me a *long time* to put it together." The children in the audience were really enjoying the show, laughing at every excuse, because it was so real. Then we stopped the show at the point of conflict. We went down to sit with the children and asked, "How are they going to solve this problem?"

At first the children were stunned and upset that we hadn't "finished the show." But when we said, "We need some ideas on what to do next," the ideas came.

1) "Teachers should hit the kids for not cleaning up." We talked about this idea and decided that no one likes to be hit.

2) "Teachers should scream at the kids." People concluded that no one likes to be screamed at.

3) "No one should clean up. Just leave all the stuff out." We talked about that and concluded that sometimes that can work but that things start getting in the way, getting lost, getting broken.

4) Finally, the solution came. "They should *all* clean up together, grownups and children." We talked about this. "Do we *like* to clean up?" No. Everybody agreed it was no fun. "Why do it, then?" The discussion continued.

After that discussion, we played out the rest of the show the way the children resolved it (#4 solution). Then the children had time to play with the puppets and do their own shows. It was fantastic! And since then, our clean-up problems have really been cut in half.

That was a good, effective conflict resolution puppet show. I could see using this method for other conflicts that came up during the day, playing them up to the point of conflict, using the words that children use—conflicts about sharing toys, dealing with bullies, mealtime scenes, put-downs. The children would be able to think of some, too!

Sometimes Puppets Aren't Necessary

At a family day organized by the Nonviolence and Children subcommittee, a playroom was set up for young people who didn't want to sit through the afternoon sessions. Some of the younger children wanted to play with the puppets that I had ready, but an older group (ages ten to twelve) that seemed to have a lot of steam of its own quickly abandoned the puppets and began setting up a skit and acting it out themselves.

The plot involved three children who were caught between a rigid, stifling school situation and a very dictatorial mother. It was a lively, melodramatic series of scenes where the older people fit into oppressive stereotypes and the younger ones were imaginative and persistent in resisting being ordered around. They plotted all kinds of nonviolent resistance, such as running away or winning the mother over with love. The rest of us settled in to watch. In spite of the simplistic nature of the story, most of the young people there were clearly absorbed and thoroughly enjoyed watching the struggle acted out.

—*Ellen Deacon*

"How to," or Goal-Wish Problem-Solving

Editor's Note: *We have encountered several step-by-step problem-solving approaches through our work with Nonviolence and Children. We have found goal-wish problem-solving to be particularly useful, and so it is described in detail below. Another useful method, "Six-Step Problem-Solving," appears in the account of work in Lansdowne Friends School, p. 55.*

Introduction

The following problem-solving process* is useful in sessions with groups to generate solutions for specific problems. The process is a highly-structured discipline which depends on the group's understanding that:

1) one person will own the problem as his or hers and the rest of the group will be used as a "brain trust" in solving the problem;

2) the other members of the group will not criticize or question the person whose problem is being worked on except to clarify information;

3) no one in the group will criticize or discuss anyone else's ideas.

One person acts as facilitator of the process for the advocate (the person whose problem is being worked on) and for the group. The advocate and facilitator roles can be rotated. The facilitator:

- encourages speaking;
- helps to clarify questions;
- writes (on big sheets of paper with crayon or marker) what is said, using the speaker's own words as closely as possible;
- watches time; and
- speeds the process with enthusiasm.

The optimum group size is eight to ten.

During the session, members of the group jot down on note paper the thoughts they don't have time to voice. These slips of paper are given to the advocate at the end of the session.

The Process

I. Identifying Problems

Note: *This is an optional step. The group may already have defined the problem it wishes to work on, in which case it must choose an advocate before beginning II, "Explaining the Problem."*

The facilitator can also ask for volunteers to outline their problems ahead of time. That way, the facilitator selects and prioritizes the problems to work on before the session begins.

A. The facilitator asks the group to brainstorm problems which it would like to work on. (Brainstorming is throwing out ideas off the top of one's head without commenting or censoring them.) The problems are not described in any detail at this point. The facilitator records the problems on a large sheet of paper so that everybody can see them.

B. With the help of the facilitator, the group decides which problems it would like to work on and puts them in the order it would like to discuss first, second, etc.

II. Explaining the Problem

A. The person who suggested the problem which is now at the top of the list becomes the advocate. The facilitator asks the advocate to give details about the problem for about three minutes, covering the following questions:

---

* This process is based in part on our own interpretation of some of the principles developed by Synectics, Inc., Cambridge, Mass., and Open Connections, Bala Cynwyd, Pa. An additional resource is a book written by the founder of Synectics, Inc., George M. Prince, *The Practice of Creativity,* Harper and Row, New York, 1970.

1. How is this a problem?
2. How is this a problem for you rather than for other people?
3. What have you already thought of to solve the problem?
4. What is an unlikely solution you can fantasize which, if it came true, would fill all your dreams?

During these three minutes the members of the group should be writing on their notepads all thoughts that come to them about how the problem might be solved.

B. The facilitator asks the advocate to state the question which he or she would most like the group to work on. The advocate does this using one phrase, starting with "how to" or an active verb. (Phrases which start with "how to" seem to engage people's minds immediately in finding solutions.) The facilitator writes this "how to" (and every other "how to" which comes later) on the large paper.

C. The group as a whole, including the advocate, makes "goal-wishes" in "how to" form about the problem question. For instance, to the problem question, "How to get friends for the child everyone hates?" wishes might include "How to have everyone discover they like the child" or "How to have the unpopular child die so everyone would be sorry." Crazy, unthinkable thoughts are ideas that may have the germ of a possible solution which our usual, more strictured thinking would censor.

III. **Processing the Problem into Possible Solutions**

A. The facilitator asks the advocate to select those ideas which seem particularly attractive, and to respond to one of them with a "specified response." (A "specified response" is made by naming at least three things which are exciting about the idea and why they are attractive and by identifying one "hole that needs to be filled" in order for the idea to become a real solution.) The facilitator records this as a balance sheet, with good ideas on one side and "holes to be filled" on the other. Thinking in terms of a balance sheet keeps us trying to solve the problem by tipping the balance.

B. The advocate formulates a "how to" question about the area which still needs to be worked on in order for the idea to become a possible solution to the problem.

C. In "how to" form, the group brainstorms possible solutions or ways that this goal-wish might be enacted.

D. The advocate comments on any ideas which are possible solutions and builds on them with the group, using "specified responses," until one or more possible solutions are found that the advocate believes can be implemented. Having more than one possible solution to a problem is preferable so that the advocate does not get frozen into "this or nothing" thinking.

E. The facilitator asks the advocate to state the concrete steps which she or he will take to implement the solution, and to set some goals about the time (tomorrow, next week) when he or she will take these steps.

F. The facilitator gives the advocate all the large sheets of recorded "how to's," itemized responses, etc. The advocate may want to ask some participants afterwards for information that was interesting but was cut off during the session because of the pressure of time.

The group can now go back to another goal-wish on the same problem or to a new problem with a new advocate.

Advantages of the Process

The advantages of this process for school faculties are that:
- it is quick;
- it generates a lot of information which can be used to solve the problem, without lecturing or having people talking at each other;
- it eliminates comparing stories, giving advice, and making remarks that make the situation seem hopeless.

Two Experiences in Goal-Wish Problem-Solving

IN SEARCH OF FAIRY GODPERSONS

*by Anne G. Toensmeier
reprinted from* Fellowship
October 1975

"You can't come to my next birthday." "I got a Slurpee and you didn't." "Then I won't be your friend." The sing-song taunts and threats, often reminiscent of my own childhood, rang in my mind as I drove into Philadelphia for a parent support group meeting. It troubled me that the pre-schoolers in our suburban neighborhood engaged in such put-downs. Our own four-year-old was learning a lot about human relations in the backyard, much of it negative.

Half an hour later, my problem was the subject of some vigorous and even fanciful group thinking. To sample a new problem-solving process, we brainstormed problems, then chose mine, a concern shared by the others.

Each of us made a "goal-wish"—some positive reversal of the problem. As these were wishes, not solutions, we could soar above practicality (how to have a fairy godperson swoop down to stop each put-down). As advocate—the problem's owner—I had to choose among goal-wishes. Realizing that put-downs both come from and cause insecurity, I chose the "how-to" that when a child is belittled, her inner voice would say, "What she says about me isn't the real me."

We brainstormed solutions aimed at this goal-wish. The variety was exciting. Again it was my role to choose two favorites and even to plot my first concrete steps. One of my choices was to have each child, after a negative incident, affirm herself and the others involved.

Exhilarated and grateful, I returned to the backyard scene with a roll of large papers under my arm—the record of the problem-solving session. I never actually unrolled it, but I have used many of the ideas, and with some success. More important is my new confidence that solutions are possible—and that I can find them.

Perhaps the children have absorbed more than I had realized. Yesterday, when Eric's feelings had been hurt, but not by them, his neighborhood friends spontaneously expressed some needed affirmation: "But you *are* a good person, Eric." "We missed you when you were on vacation." "We like you." Listening, I glowed.

46

INTERGENERATIONAL "THINK TANK"

by Ellen Deacon

At an intergenerational workshop, Chuck and I planned to do a goal-wish problem-solving session for the whole group, young and old. We explained what we were planning to do—an activity in which people could form a "think tank" group to help someone find solutions to a problem he or she was having. We asked that people with a problem with which they wanted some help tell us about it during a break and suggested that we pick the most interesting one or two to work on with the whole group watching. (We didn't have time that morning to do Step I of the process, which would have the *group* choose the problems it wanted to work on.)

Carrie, a five year old, came up during the break and said she had a problem. She felt that her teacher wouldn't give Carrie enough time to finish work during school and wouldn't cooperate with her request to take the work home. We chose Carrie's problem to work on and asked a group of about seven people to volunteer to be the "think tank," or problem-solving group, while the rest of the participants (about 25 other people) watched quietly. The small group of volunteers ranged in age from eleven to the mid-forties.

Chuck first explained about being an "advocate"—that Carrie, as the person with the problem, was the determining authority about the definition of the problem and how usable the ideas generated actually were. He cautioned that we were not looking for advice, but rather for a lot of ideas, no matter how absurd. Then he asked Carrie to explain her problem. Chuck and everyone else listened carefully. He allowed the small group to ask clarifying questions. After that he asked Carrie to put the problem into a "how-to" phrase, which he recorded on a large sheet of paper.

The small group brainstormed ideas about the problem, phrased as sentences beginning with "how-to..."; for example, "How to put giant ears on the teacher so she really hears what's happening." Chuck encouraged people not to limit their suggestions to logical or possible ideas, but to come up with "how-to's" which were as imaginative as possible. After compiling a list of about fifteen ideas,

Chuck read them all back to Carrie. Since she didn't yet read easily, he read the list to her a few times. The last time, he summarized each item as briefly as possible.

Next, Chuck encouraged Carrie to pick two or three which she liked most. (Choosing the best possible solutions is a necessary part of moving towards action on a problem. However, this often seems to be a stumbling block for the advocate. The facilitator should be gently insistent that the advocate choose two or three ideas that he or she most likes from the list, even if this seems hard to do. It is important to give the advocate plenty of space to think while communicating the expectation that a choice can be made.)

Once she had picked two or three, Chuck asked Carrie to choose the "how-to" she wanted to pursue further. She chose, "How to have another talk by myself with the teacher." Many of the older people clearly didn't think that Carrie's choice was the best one. (The subtle and not-so-subtle impulses to tell her what to do kept popping up all during the session, not only from the small group but from the observers.)

The small group began again to brainstorm, this time possible solutions to the problem, "How to have another talk with the teacher." A number of ideas were generated, and Chuck asked Carrie to pick the ones she thought would work. Then he asked her to state clearly what she intended to do, and he wrote this out in her own words on the large paper. Then he gave her all the sheets he had written up.

At several points in the process, Chuck had to insist more firmly than usual that people stifle their urges to tell Carrie what she should do. Many people, including myself, were surprised and bothered by the fact that she didn't immediately embrace the proposed solutions which involved getting her mother or some other third party to come to school to help her negotiate with the teacher. She seemed quite secure in the idea that she could work this problem out for herself. Chuck persisted in protecting her from the barrage of well-intentioned but misplaced attempts to fix things up for her. She was able to come out of the session with some ideas which truly supported her sense of her own power.

Postscript from Carrie's Mother

This was an incredible session to watch, not just because Carrie is my daughter.

She took the session in her stride and as far as I know she never specifically acted on the suggestions, but I believe her feelings toward school changed. She seemed less frustrated about not getting everything right all the time.

I think what was really significant was the *process*, the concern that Carrie felt from the group, her ability to interact with and gain help from those outside her family....

I read parts of Ellen's account to Carrie, simplifying along the way. At the end I asked her what she liked best about it. "I liked telling my problem to the people," she replied.

Each conflict situation, as any situation, is unique. It requires some new thinking; no technique can be automatically "plugged in" and be successful.

This section has described a sampling of approaches which people have used thoughtfully in conflict resolution. We hope that it serves as the beginning of a dialogue with many other people. Please let us know about your thinking, approaches, experiences and successes.

48

Competition and Community

The Manual So Far

The elements already explored in this manual—affirmation, sharing, and conflict resolution—all contribute to a nonviolent atmosphere and to a sense of supportive community. A truly supportive community includes people inspiring excellence through affirming themselves and each other. It involves people sharing their feelings, skills, and experiences. It requires that people bring their conflicts to the surface and deal with them, so that long-term difficulties do not inhibit support.

Supportive Community

While we yearn and strive for this sense of supportive community, our society does not foster it. Rather, it pits people against each other. Students compete for grades; working people compete for wages. Students are often not encouraged to work together; in fact, helping a classmate sometimes is viewed as "cheating." That mentality carries over to the workplace, where new ideas are guarded jealously.

Competition

These aspects of competition are destructive of people and of a sense of community. Competition, however, does not have to be negative. One can compete against an outside standard to improve one's skills; a runner, for instance, competes against the clock. One can compete within the context of friendship and camaraderie, where friendship is honestly more important than the achievement. Competition, or striving, in which *nobody* is put down, and in which we rejoice in our own and in others' excellence, is certainly not destructive. Competition which involves "losers" is.

Developing a Mindset

It is possible to counter the destructive aspects of competition and to foster a sense of supportive community in our own life situations. We can develop a mindset consistent with a nonviolent atmosphere; moreover, we can use processes and approaches which nurture and maintain this atmosphere. For example, Sarah Taylor's own mindset of affirmation led to her decision to change the evaluation system in her Headstart Center (p.13). The new system, in turn, created a more affirmative mindset among the staff, and therefore among the children.

49

Rest of the Manual

So far this manual has presented theory and approaches which help to build a nonviolent atmosphere and a mindset of supportive community. The rest of the manual includes actual examples-accounts of individuals and groups who have used the theory and have adapted the approaches to their own situations. These accounts and examples are categorized into four sections.

First, "Work in Lansdowne Friends School" (p. 51) and "Work in the Children's School" (p. 59) are accounts of the Nonviolence and Children Collective's presence in actual classroom situations. Lois Dorn's "Magic Meetings" and Tom Ewell's "Creating an Environment" are descriptions of these individuals' efforts in family and in school, respectively.

Next are three sections on processes, or approaches, which groups can use in working together toward establishing a nonviolent atmosphere for adults and children. Berit Lakey's "Meeting Facilitation" (p.79) outlines steps for consensual decision-making which faculties, parents and student groups can adapt and use. Karen Zaur's "Staffings" (p. 84) describes a process for teachers to think together about an individual child or classroom problem. Lois Dorn and Anne Toensmeier's "Parent Support Groups" (p.90) is an account of a series of meetings which parents (and friends of parents) can establish to provide support for themselves and each other.

Third, "Books for Young People" (p. 102) is a resource section of excellent books which step out of a destructively competitive mindset to provide alternatives in dealing with feelings, sex roles, and conflict resolution.

Finally, Marta Harrison's *For the Fun of It! Selected Cooperative Games,* the popular forerunner of this manual, is reprinted as an appendix. These games can help to form a cooperative basis of friendship in play—and they are just plain fun. Marta addresses some cogent questions at more length in her foreword, "Beyond Competition: A Search for Excellence."

The following sections contain, then, our own and others' actual experiences, processes, and resources which nurture a nonviolent atmosphere. Please let us know of your own.

Work in Lansdowne Friends School*

The School

Lansdowne Friends School is a small Quaker elementary school (K-6) in Lansdowne, Pennsylvania, a white, middle-class suburb bordering a black section of West Philadelphia. It has recently enrolled fairly equal numbers of black and white students, varying widely in family background and academic achievement. The school is noted for its small size (about 100 children) and its supportive atmosphere not only for its students but also for its teachers in their various teaching styles.

Making Arrangements

In the spring of 1973, Stephanie was looking for a school in which to develop a one-year pilot program which would include affirmation and sharing activities and would try to build cooperation and conflict-resolution skills. Lansdowne Friends, with its small size and supportive atmosphere, seemed a good place for such a program.

Through Quaker contacts, Stephanie knew Dot Lenk and Dorothy Flanagan, sixth and primary grade teachers respectively; Mary Alice Hoffman, a parent who was deeply involved in the school; and the principal, Nancy Wilkinson. They all welcomed Stephanie's proposal for the program, especially since it seemed to be an opportunity to emphasize contemporary Quakerism in the school. The program was funded through Quaker sources.

Over the summer, definite plans were made. The program would start in Dot Lenk's sixth grade class, with Mary Alice Hoffman helping Dot and Stephanie. Stephanie hoped that in a few months the sixth graders might be ready to work as facilitators for a program with Dorothy Flanagan's first and second graders (see "On Combining Ages," p. 58).

Program in Sixth Grade

September through November

In September, Stephanie met and observed the sixth grade class to become acquainted with it, and Dot Lenk announced the program to the parents at a "Back to School" night. Also in September, Chuck Esser and Keith Miller, two men with experience in teaching and nonviolence training, joined the Nonviolence and Children staff. In October, the program began.

On Wednesday mornings from 11:00 to 11:45, the three Nonviolence and Children staff people worked with Dot and Mary Alice and the sixth graders. Since the class was small, the trainers rotated so that two of them were present each week, making up a total of four adults and thirteen children. At the end of the session the students left for lunch, while the adults ate together in the classroom. The sessions were planned to precede such a time, when the adults would be able to get together to evaluate the session, think about the following week, and discuss concerns which Dot had about the class or about particular students.

At Thanksgiving time, Stephanie departed for a previously-planned two-month trip to India. Chuck and Keith continued the program for the rest of the year, with Stephanie substituting when necessary after she returned. The greater continuity was easier both for the facilitators and for the children.

In addition to the sessions and lunch meetings, Chuck, Keith and Stephanie went on class trips throughout the year. They found these trips to be a good time to get to know the children and adults in other contexts than the classroom, and Dot found it helpful to have them along as extra adult friends.

The beginning weeks were devoted to building a basis of trust and safety into the session through songs, cooperative games and sharing circles. Two representative session plans and evaluations went as follows:

* A briefer description of the Nonviolence and Children Program at Lansdowne and of the Program's basic approaches appeared in an article by Stephanie Judson entitled "Nonviolence and Children: Interim Reflections," *Fellowship*, October 1974. Reprints (20 cents) are available from Friends Peace Committee, 1515 Cherry St., Philadelphia, PA 19102, and from Fellowship of Reconciliation, Box 271, Nyack, NY 10960.

FIRST SESSION PLAN

Stephanie and Chuck facilitating

Purpose:

To begin building a sense of community and an expectation that everybody would get a chance to participate in our sessions.

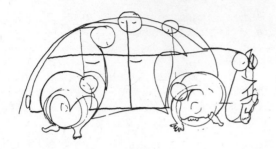

Plan:

Stephanie will introduce session, explain what will happen.

Introductions: people divide into pairs and interview each other on—

    a) What do you like to do after school?

    b) What was your favorite part of the class camping trip?

Then people introduce their partners to the whole class.

Cooperative game, "Let's Build a Machine" (see Games, p. G-18). Chuck will facilitate.

EVALUATION OF FIRST SESSION

+ *(Good Things)*	**—** *(Things That Weren't Good and/or Need Changing)*	↗ *(Ways to Improve, or Things to Keep in Mind)*
Introductions went well—lots of good memories and good sharing.		
Dot had suggested camping trip as a good interview topic since it was such a community-building experience, and community-building was part of today's purpose.		Be sure to be in touch with Dot about sharing topics.
	Brian's feelings were hurt when Sally shared an embarrassing incident from the camping trip, when Brian talked in his sleep.	Sally probably wasn't trying to hurt or make fun of Brian. She saw the incident as funny and wanted to laugh about it again. Later on, more on theory of put-ups and put-downs needs to be worked on.
"Let's Build a Machine"—fun. People seemed to warm up to it.		
	Things seemed to fizzle at end, without a definite sense of closure.	Let's get into a habit of some kind of closing circle.

52

SEVENTH SESSION PLAN

Keith and Stephanie facilitating

Purpose:

To continue to encourage children to share experiences, ideas and feelings.

To begin to introduce sharing unpleasant experiences in a safe way.

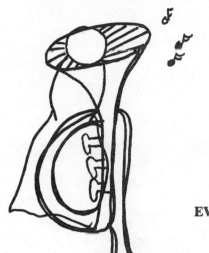

Plan:

Excitement-sharing, Stephanie facilitating.

Cooperative game, "Sue's Game" (a values clarification activity; see Games, p. G-19), Stephanie will facilitate.

Random Memory Circle (see Sharing, p. 24). Keith will facilitate. People can respond as they wish (not in turn this time) by briefly recounting their experiences.

Closing Circle: "My favorite dessert is..." Stephanie will facilitate.

Some games if we need them: "One Word Story" (p. G-18), "Pass the Mask" (p. G-26), "Rainstorm" (p. G-14).

EVALUATION OF SEVENTH SESSION

+ (Good Things)	— (Things That Weren't Good, and/or Need Changing)	↗ (Ways to Improve, or Things to Keep in Mind)
"Sue's Game" a great success—seems to be an affirming thing all-around and stretches the imagination.		Think of other things for "Sue's Game" (e.g., if you were a type of weather...); maybe do this again later in the year.
	Some put-downs, distracting comments throughout the session.	Time now to work on put-downs and also to remind firmly.
Unpleasant memories—Keith did terrific blend of pleasant, funny (i.e., slightly embarrassing) and more unpleasant memories.		We can plan to move into sharing circles, when each person gets a chance to share on one theme.
	People were jumpy at end.	A better closing would be an active song game after so much sitting and sharing. We need to be aware of people's needs, and be flexible in our planning.

The children enjoyed the sessions during the first months of the program and seemed to be sharing their feelings openly. An evaluation/discussion, which Dot Lenk held during a school day when the Nonviolence and Children staff was not present, confirmed that the students looked forward to the sessions and had a good understanding of their purpose.

Flexible Planning

Keith, Chuck and I worked out a good method of planning sessions. At the planning meeting each person had a turn to think out loud about the coming session while another recorded all the ideas in the lesson plan notebook. Comments and discussion weren't allowed until each of us had taken a turn. That way we had a lot of ideas clearly before us. Often we'd find that we all had the same general ideas and could recognize a consensus forming. Other times, it seemed that we had sparked each other's thinking by this process, and excellent ideas emerged from one of us.

After we'd listened to each other, we usually formulated a plan fairly easily and quickly by considering all the recorded ideas. This method gave us the benefit of the thinking of each individual of the group together in working out a final plan.

Most important in planning was an emphasis on remaining flexible and an agreement to do what made sense to us at any given time. We could have a fantastic plan and, when we arrived for a session, discover it was totally inappropriate. So we'd scrap the plan, pay attention to where the students were, and adapt.

A good example of this happened one winter Wednesday. Shortly before Keith and Chuck arrived, Dot Lenk had learned that her husband had cancer, and she had left school for the day, frightened and tearful. The plan for the day—to explain in more detail our general philosophy and "where we're coming from"—was obviously inappropriate.

Chuck and Keith listened to the children tell what had happened and acknowledged that they were upset and scared. As it happened, a woman visiting our session that day had been struggling with her own cancer for a few years. She shared her experiences with the children, remarking that today she was able to be right there in the class and functioning well. After the students had a chance to talk more and ask the visitor some questions, Keith and Chuck quickly moved into the "Corners Game" (see Games, p. G-19). It was a good move: once they'd dealt with their initial feelings, the students could move around actively and think about something else. When Dot returned, she would give them more information about the particular situation and discuss it more. There would be plenty of time for that—but right now, the facilitators did the appropriate thing—and scrapped the plan.

—*Stephanie Judson*

54

A PROBLEM IN DECISION-MAKING

During the first months of the program, the facilitators were particularly bothered by the students' clamoring to be chosen for tasks that needed doing (e.g., "Pick me first!" "Oh, me!" while waving hands in adults' faces). Since neither the facilitators nor the teachers nor the students had established a method of choosing, the clamoring continued to be a problem week after week.

At the beginning of one session shortly after Stephanie had left for India, Chuck and Keith encountered this clamoring again. Instead of continuing with the plan for the day, they decided to take this problem as a focus. Chuck drew on his knowledge of a problem-solving method,* and the session went as follows:

"Step 1: Defining the Problem in Terms of Needs"

Chuck and Keith explained to the class that they were very frustrated by the clamoring and demanding every time somebody had to be chosen. They emphasized that this was their own problem and these were their own feelings and that they hoped the students, Dot, and Mary Alice would work with them to find a solution.

"Step 2: Generating Possible Solutions"

Everybody suggested ways to decide who would be chosen. All the possible solutions were recorded on the blackboard, with no debate or discussion until everyone had finished making suggestions.

"Step 3: Evaluating and Testing the Various Solutions"

Each solution was reviewed and discussed for its various merits and drawbacks. Any solution with which more than two people disagreed was crossed off the blackboard and rejected as a possibility. At least one person disagreed with every solution. There were only two solutions with which only one or two people disagreed.

"Step 4: Deciding on a Mutually Acceptable Solution"

The two solutions which were still in the running were "playing spin the bottle" and "going in alphabetical order." As it happened, Dot Lenk was the only person who disagreed with the solution of spinning the bottle. As the two remaining solutions were further discussed, Dot agreed that she would try "spin the bottle." (See her anecdote, "Spin the Bottle!?")

* "The Six Steps in Method III Problem Solving Process" from *Teacher Effectiveness Training Teacher Notebook*, copyright 1972 by Thomas Gordon, reproduced by special permission.

"Step 5: Implementing the Solution"

The group agreed that the next time somebody had to be chosen to go first in an activity, or to do a special task, the class would form a circle and either Chuck or Keith would spin a bottle in the center. Whoever "won" that time (i.e., whomever the bottle was pointing to) would spin the bottle the next time.

The group was eager to try this solution. So Keith and Chuck proposed that the session end with a game which required somebody to go first. A bottle was produced, and the solution was implemented immediately.

"Step 6: Evaluating the Solution"

Usually, a time is set to try the method chosen and the method is evaluated at the end of the time (e.g., three days, a week). In this case, the success of the solution was obvious and no evaluation was done. However, it would have been a good idea to evaluate anyway so that everybody could get into the habit of expecting an evaluation in case they used the process for another problem. Not all solutions are as successful, especially first time around, and knowing that a time for evaluation and possible changes is coming makes trying a solution more palatable.

"Spin the Bottle!?"

I originally objected to "spin the bottle" because it brought to mind for me all those silly party games with sexual overtones. I thought the class would go into hysterical giggles every time we spun that bottle.

Later, I realized that was *my* preconception. The students never once giggled at the idea when we were brainstorming about it with Chuck and Keith, or later, for that matter. I don't know whether they'd even heard of "spin the bottle" as a kissing game.

—*Dot Lenk*

Reflections on This Problem-Solving Approach

The solution of spinning the bottle to choose somebody is a creative one which the adults in the group probably would not have chosen on their own —or even considered. The method we used allowed this solution to emerge. More significantly, the method provided a way for the whole group to agree on a solution. Therefore, everybody felt that she or he had a stake in making the solution work.

From that session on, a deeper sense of community and involvement grew within the sessions. Also, the class used "spin the bottle" during the regular school day for the rest of the year.

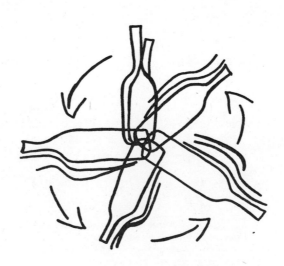

December through March

Singing, cooperative games and sharing circles continued during these months. In addition, in an effort to counter the put-downs which were a regular occurrence in the class, Keith and Chuck decided to focus on affirmation exercises. They explained briefly the reasons for the importance of affirmation. The entire group, adults and children, did affirmation silhouettes (see Affirmation, p. 7), affirming two people each week. The silhouettes, with comments, were posted in the hallway.

The structured affirmation activity provided a dramatic contrast to the negative comments the students were used to giving each other informally. The exercise seemed to heighten the class's consciousness about just how destructive put-downs are.

Henry's affirmation was a good example of this. He often criticized his classmates. During the affirmation time in the Wednesday session, Henry found it almost impossible to say anything good about his classmates without a sarcastic qualifier. When it was Henry's turn to be affirmed, Keith and Chuck held their breath and crossed their fingers. Would Henry receive the same?

Each person in the class affirmed Henry in some thoughtful, genuine way! In the evaluation after the session, the adults agreed that the students had understood the value of affirmation more than they had anticipated. And indeed, Henry began to stop putting people down as he discovered that he really was likeable. The destructive cycle was interrupted.

Sharing circles continued to be another important part of the sessions. The sharing times were most memorable when they focused on a concern at hand (e.g., fears about going to junior high school, thoughts after receiving the news that Dot Lenk's husband had cancer, remembering at Christmas time about when we didn't get a particular present we wanted). Favorite cooperative games included "Elephant-Palm Tree" and "Swat!" (see Games, pp. G-13, G-12).

April and May

The affirmation silhouettes were completed by this time. Keith and Chuck conducted other affirmation activities, sharing circles, and cooperative and listening games.

Repeating these activities was valuable. The students seemed to explore new aspects and ideas each time they carried out an activity. They looked forward to each session, too, peering out the window as they anticipated Keith's and Chuck's arrival.

In retrospect, however, it would have been appropriate to do more problem-solving and conflict resolution with that class. By the end of the year, some respected students were coming up to Chuck and Keith to let them know about a conflict or a problem in the classroom. This was a tacit request for help in dealing with these problems.

Thoughts on Problem-solving

During the year we were working in Lansdowne Friends, we were searching for useful information, tools, and approaches for problem-solving with elementary age students. We found some that year—the "6-Point Problem Solving" (p. 55) is a good example.

The following autumn (1974) we asked the staff of Quaker Project on Community Conflict to come down from New York to meet with us for a skill-sharing session. We were particularly interested in their work with puppetry and role-playing in explaining conflicts to children. Given what we know now, here's a scenario showing how we might have approached problem-solving with the Lansdowne sixth grade.

Keith and Chuck, with Mary Alice's and Dot's help, present a two-minute skit portraying a conflict situation. The students divide into small groups to discuss the situation and come up with a solution. Everybody regathers and each small group presents its solution, with discussion by the whole group of each presentation. (For more on this, see Conflict Resolution, p. 41.)

Conflicts *outside* the classroom (e.g., a store manager bullying a child, younger children being harassed by older children on the way home from school) would certainly be best to start with. Conflicts *within* the classroom are riskier for the class to explore, but with some background or build-up and the affirmation and sharing skills they already had acquired that year, they would have been possible.

—*Stephanie Judson*

57

On Combining Ages...

"Helping relationships" and cross-age education, in which older students become teachers of younger children, had interested me ever since graduate school. I thought the concept would apply in two areas. First, it would break down age segregation. It didn't make sense to me that fourth graders, or nine-year-olds, for instance, saw only each other and their teachers all day. Second, it would give older students a chance to feel important and useful by helping younger ones. It might even help some older students who were having trouble academically to learn by teaching.

Originally, I had wanted to develop a year-long program at Lansdowne Friends which would build up to a cross-age component. What a satisfying "first" for the Nonviolence and Children Program in two areas! We'd never had a year-long program, and *nobody* had ever done a cross-age "affectively-oriented" program before.

I spent a lot of time over the summer learning about cross-age education. The Philadelphia Board of Education Affective Education Department was becoming involved in it, so I went to some of their planning meetings, read a lot, and thought some. I planned that the fall would be spent in developing a program with the Lansdowne sixth graders, and that after I got back from India the sixth graders would work with second and first graders. The adults at Lansdowne seemed willing to give it a try, and I was excited.

But it wasn't right, and it didn't happen. As Dot Lenk said later, the idea "died on the vine." Keith and Chuck joined the staff after I'd made all of these plans. They didn't seem as interested in cross-age education as I was—I'm not sure I even articulated my plans clearly to them. More important, the sixth graders got deeply involved in their own Nonviolence and Children program and obviously were not ready to switch to something else.

An interesting footnote: The next fall the Nonviolence and Children staff did a series of sessions at Friends Select School in a first and second grade classroom. Three girls who had gone on to seventh grade there from Lansdowne Friends the year before eagerly volunteered to help in the first and second grade classrooms. These Lansdowne "alumnae" helped tutor the younger children, worked with gymnastics and organized games at recess. Though they were not purely "affective, nonviolent" helping relationships, they were certainly a great help for the teacher and made the students feel important and useful in a new school. So it did happen—in its own time and way.

—*Stephanie Judson*

FOLLOW UP AND CARRY THROUGH

The following school year, Dot Lenk and Mary Alice Hoffman carried on a weekly program with the new sixth grade class, based on the program of the previous year. Following the same basic approaches, they concluded that they reached "at least in part" all of their goals. Dot found that as the classroom teacher she could build on the experiences of the weekly program during the regular school day. She could also plan the weekly sessions knowing more specifically "what was happening" with the students at the time. Mary Alice's presence as a person from the " 'outside' meant that the program did not get put aside in favor of more academic subjects." In evaluating their two year experience, Mary Alice and Dot emphasized the importance of gearing affirmation and other activities to the needs and level of each particular class.

The Nonviolence and Children staff tried to keep in touch with Dot and Mary Alice as their program proceeded throughout the year, and also returned for a one-day faculty workshop at the school. Two years later, the Program continued to relate to Lansdowne Friends, with Karen Zaur and Marta Harrison going out to help with some problem-solving in a staff meeting.

Work in the Children's School

Editor's Note: *We have written the account of our work at the Children's School mainly as a compilation of session plans, evaluations, memos, and anecdotes.*

Many people have asked us "Just exactly what did you do each week in a school?" Including the session plans is an attempt to answer this question and to outline what we did. The plans are not, of course, a magic blueprint, but rather a brief account of what seemed to make sense in one particular school situation.

Evaluations help us to review, appreciate, and critique our work, and to be in touch with and appreciate each other. The evaluations in this account are lengthy and largely unedited, in an attempt to provide a sense of what went on in longer evaluation sessions.

The purpose of anecdotes and memos is self-explanatory. Through them we've tried to indicate the richness of our experience at the Children's School, and to share our thinking from it.

The School

The Children's School is a small alternative public school in a racially and economically mixed residential neighborhood near the center of Philadelphia. Opened in 1970, the school houses a Parent Cooperative nursery school, an informal classroom for five to seven year olds which is administered by the principal of the nearby Samuel Powel Elementary School, and the office of the Powelton-Mantua Cooperative Education Fund. It was the Fund, begun by a group of parents trying to start an open classroom elementary school within the public school system, which organized and continues to own and maintain the Children's School. The Nonviolence and Children Program worked in the vertically-grouped kindergarten, first and second grade class of 30 students.

Karen Zaur and Jessica Agre were the teachers for the K-2 classroom in 1974-75. Excellent teachers with extensive experience in open education, they firmly believed that the most important things for a child in their class was to develop a strong sense of self-worth. They also believed that open education allowed children to learn effectively. Their open classroom was an orderly, enjoyable environment; the children responded to Karen and Jessica's high and clearly-stated expectations that the students take responsibility for themselves and their own behavior.

Genesis of the Program at the Children's School

Marianna Cayten asked the Nonviolence and Children Collective to join her at the Children's School for the 1974-75 year. Marianna, whose daughter attended the school, had volunteered in the nursery class the previous year, using many of the approaches of the Nonviolence and Children Program. The collective members were eager for the opportunity to work in such a public school, and to work with younger children than we had previously. We were also excited about working with Marianna. She could share her broad knowledge and perceptions of alternative schooling within the public school system with us, and we could share our skills with her.

60

After observing in the K-2 classrooms, talking with Karen and Jessica, and then meeting with the parents to get their approval, Chuck Esser and Ellen Forsythe from the collective began working with Marianna in November, 1974. They continued to work with her class for an hour every Tuesday morning until June, 1975.

Session Plans

The sessions usually began with the whole group together for singing and stories. Then the class divided into three small groups for activities around the theme of the day (affirmation, feelings, problem-solving, etc.), reconvening as a whole group for a song or game or story at the end of the hour. Lunch followed the session. The five adults ate together and evaluated the morning.

Goals of the Children's School Program

For the students: to help them become more affirmative of each other and themselves, more aware of their feelings, more creative in solving problems.

For Karen and Jessica: to support them, share with them and learn from them.

For Marianna: to support her in her continuing efforts, to learn from her about neighborhood public alternative education, to provide an ongoing experience in Nonviolence and Children work.

For Ellen (then a new collective member): to allow her to gain experience with our program.

For Chuck: to gain experience in being with younger children, to learn about excellent open classroom education.

For the NVC Collective: to gain experience in a public school situation in an environment we appreciate.

For all of us: to enjoy ourselves and the children while doing this!

SESSION 1

Large group:

Singing "Do Your Ears Hang Low?"

Small groups:

Jack-in-the-Box Introductions (see Games, p. G-9).

Who Can I Meet Today? Children volunteer to be interviewed. Facilitator interviews each with a couple of light questions and asks others for questions they'd like to ask. Interviewee sits on lap or snuggled up to facilitator. (See Sharing, p. 22.)

Large group:

Playing "Touch Blue" (see Games, p. G-10)

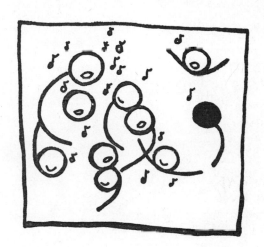

SESSION 2

Large group:

Singing, "A Woonie Koonie Cow"

Small groups:

Leaders and children go over rules for meeting. Karen and Jessica had established two basic rules for meetings: 1) The meeting begins with everybody sitting in a circle. 2) One person talks at a time.

Who Can I Meet Today? (continued).

Feeling Faces. People suggest various emotions. Everybody makes a face representing the suggested emotion.

Large group:

Singing "Do Your Ears Hang Low?"

SESSION 3

Large group:

Singing "If You're Happy and You Know It"

Small groups:

What Makes You Happy? "Think about something that makes you happy." "Show us what your face looks like when you're happy." "Share with the group what makes you happy."

Who Can I Meet Today? (continued). Today a child also introduces the adult in the group in a similar fashion.

Large group:

Singing "Do Your Ears Hang Low?"

61

Beginning Affirmation and Thinking About Feelings

Ellen, Chuck and Marianna perform a puppet show from the book, *Tears of the Dragon* (see Books, p. 104).

SESSION 4

Large group:

Singing "A Woonie Koonie Cow"

Small groups:

Who Can I Meet Today? (Finish interviews if anybody didn't have a turn.)

Review rules for meeting.

Begin Class Books about feelings (see Sharing, p. 25). Draw a picture of yourself when you are happy, or of an animal you think of when you're happy.

Large group:

Singing "If You're Happy and You Know It"

SESSIONS 7-8
Working with Puppets

SESSION 7

Large group:

Singing "Do Your Ears Hang Low?"

Small groups:

Making sock puppets. Each puppet "says something."

(No large group ending)

SESSION 5

Large group:

Listening to the recording, "It's All Right to Cry," while people gather. When everybody is settled, it's played again and people sing along. (See Books, *Free to Be You and Me*, p. 109.)

Small groups:

Excitement-sharing (see Affirmation, p. 6). Leader reads story, *Grownups Cry, Too* (see Books, p. 106). People share about "the times I cry and feel like crying and times I've seen grownups cry."

SESSION 8

Large group:

Playing "Musical Laps" (see Games, p. G-16)

Small groups:

Affirmation with puppets. (Leader explains that it's important for puppets to feel good in order to work and play well.) Everybody says something he or she likes about their own puppet. Puppet turns to the one next to it and "says" something it would like them to do together.

Large group:

Singing "If You're Happy and You Know It"

Large group:

Dancing "The Hokey Pokey"

SESSIONS 9-10
Feeling Sad

SESSION 9

Large group:

Singing "If You're Happy and You Know It... If You're Sad and You Know It"

Small groups:

Class Books (continued). "Make a picture of a time when you were sad. Share your picture with the group. We'll save them to put into the Class Book on feelings."

Large group:

Singing another chorus of "If You're Sad and You Know It"

SESSION 10

Large group:

Marianna reads *I Want My Mama*, by Marjorie Weinman Sharmat, Harper & Row, New York, 1974.

Small groups:

Sharing pictures. Everybody holds a picture drawn last week and has a chance to tell about it. "You can ask one question about each person's picture."

"Tell us about another time you were sad, or saw someone else sad." "How did you know that person was sad?"

Large group:

Playing "Head, Shoulders, Knees and Toes" (see Games, p. G-20)

SESSIONS 11-13
More on Affirmation, Feelings, Puppetry

SESSION 11

Large group:

Playing "Touch Blue"

Small groups:

Leader reads *The Quarreling Book* (see Books, p. 108). People then act out the story, using puppets.

Affirmation circle with puppets. Puppets say what they like about the people holding them.

Large group:

Plays "Do This, Do This" (a cooperative version of Simon Says, in which nobody is "out").

SESSION 12

Large group:

Playing "Zap Around the Circle." Going quickly around, each person says one thing (in one or two words) that he or she likes about winter.

Small groups:

Class Books (continued). "Draw a picture of you, doing something you like to do."

Large group:

Dancing "The Hokey Pokey"

SESSION 13

Large group:

Excitement-sharing

Small groups:

Singing "A Woonie Koonie Cow"

Puppet interviews. Each person wears his or her puppet. Puppet "interviews" another person, as in Sessions 1-3.

Large group:

Singing "Do Your Ears Hang Low?"

MID-TERM EVALUATION

Editor's Note: *After the 13th session, the five adults involved in the Nonviolence and Children sessions—Ellen, Marianna, Karen, Chuck, and Jessica—met for a "mid-term" evaluation. The notes from this meeting follow.*

What's Been Good So Far?

Jessica: You do things that we believe in, and since you're doing them, we're more apt to do them the rest of the time. For instance, Karen and I have put together those class books on feelings, and read them to the class a few times.

I like the idea of having sock puppets in the room for constant use.

It's nice for the kids, and for us, to have some other people consistently coming into the classroom. Our weekly evaluations with you are thoughtful, and you affirm us—that makes us feel really good. Your program focusses on THE MOST important area, feeling good about ourselves. Having you around helps keep it up during the times you aren't here.

The kids' silliness around you in the beginning of the year has gone.

Karen: You have used puppets in ways that never occurred to me. We've always just had puppets sitting around our room.

Chuck is the only man who comes into this classroom on a regular basis. It's a real addition to have him.

Marianna: Working with the puppets has been really good. The children went beyond my expectations. For me, watching the children listen to each other, and hearing them express the feelings has been special. It also brings me in touch with [my daughter] Cara's classroom.

Chuck: We've learned lots by working in this school and with this age group. Seeing the success of our work is helping us to develop long-range thinking. We're becoming more spontaneous and flexible. The children are requiring that! Most of the children relate to us, and seem to enjoy us, though a few opt out. We're having fun!

This has created an opportunity for Ellen and Marianna to be confident in doing things on their own.

Ellen: I like doing this evaluation. It's great to listen to you all!

What Needs To Be Changed?
What Do We Need More Of?

Jessica: More work on negative feelings and more affirmation! You can expand the work with puppets even more—it seems to be a good way of role-playing for children this age. Role-playing has been one of the most valuable things I've done in my life, but it's too complicated for children this age, I think.

Some time it would be good to deal with scary things, like going to the hospital.

Karen: I'd like us to be more consistent, using on a weekly basis the evaluation form we're using right now. It'd save time and help us to focus more.

Marianna: It would be helpful to me if during our planning and evaluation we spelled out more specifically what our goals are for what we're doing that day.

Chuck: I think we've developed a good format. We've been developing community spirit, the children have been talking about how they feel, and they've been building a feeling vocabulary. There's lots of affirmation. We just need to do *more* of this as a basis for moving into conflict resolution.

We should do more to help the children see and perceive the difference between the negative way that people act sometimes, and the way people really are. People really are loving, caring, zestful—children need that information, and need to be able to see the differences.

Ellen: I'd like to spend more time during our evaluations sharing about substantive things. For instance, it would be helpful to me if we discussed how we communicate our own needs to children and how we react to children who are letting their feelings out.

64

SESSION 14
Talking About Death

SESSION 14

Large group:

Singing "I Sat Next to the Duchess at Tea"

A close friend of Chuck, Ellen and Marianna, along with an acquaintance of theirs, had drowned in a canoeing accident three days before. They explained to the class briefly what had happened and how they were feeling and that they might cry during the session.

Small groups:

Leader reads *The Tenth Good Thing About Barney* (see Books, p. 107).

Children discuss dying, sharing feelings and stories.

Large group:

Singing "Do Your Ears Hang Low?"

SESSIONS 15-17

More on Affirmation

SESSION 15

Large group:

Playing "Pru-ee" (see Games, p. G-13)

Small groups:

Excitement-sharing

I'm Going on a Trip, Taking With Me Something I Like About Myself (see Affirmation, p. 7)

Large group:

Singing "Three Blue Pigeons" (see Games, p. G-29)

SESSION 16

Large group:

Singing "A Woonie Koonie Cow"

Small groups:

Theater Activities. Leader explains that we'll be doing a lot of silent things outdoors today, like theater exercises and "gymcraftics." In pairs, people make body sculptures without talking. Then each pair is asked to fit into the whole group structure, pair by pair. (See Karen's description of this day in Games section, p. G-17.) Partners affirm each other ("Whisper something you liked about doing the sculptures with your partner").

Large group:

Playing "Mirroring" (see Games, p. G-17)

SESSION 17

Large group:

Singing "Do Your Ears Hang Low?"

Ellen talks about put-downs and put-ups. Everybody puts-up (affirms) Karen.

Small groups:

Affirmation Circle. Going around the circle, each person is affirmed by three or four others in the group (continue in next session).

Large group:

Singing "I Sat Down With the Duchess at Tea"

Children's Ability to Affirm Thoughtfully

At the Children's School (ages 5,6,7), we began affirmations with the assumption we'd been making all along that many children would affirm what we adults viewed as superficial things. We expected a number of "I like your red sneakers" and were prepared to accept that kind of affirmation as really valid from a five year old. Red sneakers are very important at that age; they certainly were for me! But the children thought about what they said more than we gave them credit for at first. They said "You dress well" to those who cared about how they dressed, and "You have sloppy sneakers" to the children who liked to be sloppy.

Jonathan had a hard time with affirmation, and we thought that he was being silly or smartalecky when he said "I like your smelly socks" to another child. But Karen and Jessica told us afterward that Jonathan really did like that smell.

—Ellen Forsythe

"Men Don't Hug!"

During one of the sessions, Chuck was hugging a lot of people. Daryll got very angry, announcing loudly that a man isn't supposed to do that. Chuck responded by hugging Daryll and continued the session with lots more hugs.

By the end of the session Daryll had entered in, too. He was hugging other children and being hugged himself. As Chuck was leaving Daryll came up and said, "Chuck, nobody has hugged you, you need a hug," and proceeded to give him one.

—Ellen Forsythe

Problem-Solving with Puppets

In October, when Ellen and Chuck and Marianna described the program to the parent group, Jessica and I were especially excited about the problem-solving, which they had demonstrated with puppets. A few days later we used sock puppets to deal with a recurring lunchtime problem. The scene we presented: a child, after getting her lunch and sitting down at a table near her friend John, decides that she needs to go to the bathroom. When she returns, someone else is sitting in her seat. The dialogue at this point ran something like this: "I was sitting there." "Well, you got up." "But my lunch is there." "But you left the seat." "It's really my place because I was there first." "How was I supposed to know that?" "But I sat there because I wanted to sit near John." "Well, I want to sit near John, too." We had a great time hamming it up and the children loved seeing us being silly and having such a good time "fighting" with each other. When we asked them for help in solving the problem, they came up with thoughtful ideas, showing they could see several sides to the story and a variety of acceptable answers. After a short discussion, everyone seemed agreed we should end the skit by acting out the suggestion that John offer to pull up another chair so the characters could "both sit there."

—Karen Zaur

SESSION 18

Large group:

Singing "A Baby Bumble Bee"

Puppet Show with Chuck and Marianna: "Can I Play, Too?" (see anecdote, "Puppets and Conflict")

Children offer solutions.

Small groups:

Affirmation Circle (continued from last session, for children who didn't have a turn being affirmed)

Conflict resolution with puppets. Children describe a problem, puppets act it out.

Large group:

Story. Chuck tells the story of "Cold Pricklies and Warm Fuzzies" (adapted from *A Fairy Tale* by Claude Steiner, Grove Press, Inc., New York).

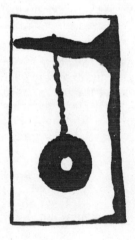

SESSION 19 (*Led by Marianna, Jessica and Karen. Ellen and Chuck were out of town.*)

Large group:

Tire Swing Show. Marianna, Karen and Jessica act out the recurring dispute of who gets to sit on the tire swing.

Small groups:

Discussion. Children discuss possible solutions and act them out.

Large group:

Dancing "The Hokey Pokey"

SESSION 20

Large group:

Singing "The Ole Family Toothbrush"

Small groups:

Excitement-sharing

Personal conflicts and resolution. "Describe a problem you have had, and get someone to act it out with you."

Large group:

Story. Chuck recounts the tale of *John, John Twilliger* (see Books, p. 105).

The Tire Swing

A favorite attraction at recess was the tire swing at the Children's School playground lot. Two children could sit in a heavy suspended tire, while a third pushed. It was a great piece of equipment, and there were always more than three children at a time who wanted to use it. Invariably, one child would get off to take a turn pushing, and a fourth would seize the opportunity to jump on before the person who had been pushing had a chance.

The usual bickering would follow. "It was *my* turn to sit on the swing!" "Who says?" "I do!" "I was pushing!" "But I want to swing, too!"

It was another good opportunity for the grownups to act it out and to mimic the argument. Marianna, Jessica and I decided to do this...too bad that Chuck and Ellen weren't able to be there that day to see us! We had another fine time "hamming." This time we divided into small groups afterwards to talk about it, and to come up with possible solutions. Once again, these children had a lot of thoughtful possibilities. And lo and behold! the tire swing situation actually improved.

—Karen Zaur

A Teller of Tales

Chuck discovered the fun of telling his own version of stories. He'd choose a book that appealed to him and seemed appropriate for the day. After reading it thoroughly to himself the night before, he'd arrive at the school with the story in his mind. The tale evolved with drama, and originality.

"And what do you think happened next?" he'd ask at an exciting point.

Some child would jump up, wide-eyed, and respond. Whatever the answer, Chuck incorporated it into the story.

With a deep, grumbly voice and a shy, high-pitched one, as well as several others in between, dramatic gestures and great humor, Chuck had everybody enraptured —including himself.

—*Karen Zaur*

Puppets and Conflict

Marianna and I did a demonstration today at the beginning of the session at the Children's School to show how we'd be using puppets in small groups. We wore puppets as we demonstrated two children fighting over blocks. Some of the children thoughtfully brought over real blocks so that the puppets would have something to fight over. After the demonstration with the whole group, we broke into small groups to go to work. Two girls in my group started playing with the blocks as we split up. Before we were able to start again, they were hitting each other, each claiming that the other had wrecked her structure.

I quickly gave them puppets, and they had the puppets hit each other for awhile. Soon they started laughing. We stopped and discussed what had happened. One of the girls remarked, "Sometimes you get into fights even with your best friend."

I think that using puppets to go into a conflict that is already happening may be very effective. But it will *not* be orderly. Working with puppets on conflict must bring feelings to the surface. As a facilitator, I must keep asking questions in order to let the feelings be expressed, not repressed. Therefore, I can't insist on quiet and order at a time like that.

—*Chuck Esser*

Chuck suggested that Sarah and Debbie use puppets to work out a fight they were having over some blocks. In the discussion that followed, the subject of hating came up. Sarah was quick to point out that "We don't *really* hate each other, we just hate each other right now!" Debbie agreed.

I had a sense they were reassuring Chuck that they wouldn't let this fight get in the way of their friendship. At the same time they were also reassuring each other of that fact. Letting that kind of discussion follow a 'fight' seems really important.

—*Karen Zaur*

After an explanation of put-ups and put-downs, we went on to do some affirmations. Sarah and Debbie, good friends, had just had a fight. It was Sarah's turn to affirm Debbie.

Sarah: Debbie, I like you because you let me take care of your scratched face.

Debbie: It's nothing. You only wash it with soapy water.

Sarah: That's a put-down and it makes me feel bad.

—*Ellen Forsythe*

68

SESSION 21

Large group:

Party! with cookies and milk and a presentation of the affirmation books the class made for each of the Nonviolence and Children staff members. We look at the books, sing some of our favorite songs, and everybody plays "This Is a Hug, This Is a Kiss" (see Games, p. G-12).

Mitch

When Mitch first came to the Children's School he had an extremely difficult time making physical contact with anyone, even when he was hurt. Over a two year period we noticed that he was gradually building trust in adults and children at school. Any clear-cut sign of affection from him was an exciting event. Once, on a walk to the zoo at the end of his first year, we suddenly realized he was walking along hand in hand with another child. Wow! (Since we don't ask the children to walk in straight lines with partners, this was purely by choice.)

Another one of those "wow" times was at the last session the NVC people spent with us. We had thought that Mitch in particular would benefit from the activities Ellen, Chuck and Marianna planned over the year. How great it would be for him to increase the number of trusting relationships he had with adults! At this final session they taught us to play "This Is a Hug, This Is a Kiss." Mitch was sitting next to Marianna, and when it was his turn he very happily and naturally gave her a kiss and got one back from her. How exciting to see him feeling safe and loving. A hug for the people who taught us that game!

—*Karen Zaur*

Special Goodbyes

Long before the final session that Marianna, Chuck and Ellen spent with us, it became clear that we all wanted to do something special for them before they stopped coming. One Tuesday I shot a few roles of black and white film of them in the classroom. Later the children used the pictures along with their own drawings and messages to compile a book for each of

them. On that last morning in May we surprised them with a party. It was a lovely time spent sharing the books we had made for them, singing the songs we had sung together, having cookies and milk together and playing "This Is a Hug, This Is a Kiss"...followed by lots more hugs and kisses as we said good-bye.

—*Karen Zaur*

69

When Mommy Comes to School

Usually the day that a child's parent comes to school to be in the classroom is a difficult but special day for the child. In the Children's School, the child is always allowed to be with his or her parent but often feels very possessive anyway. Lots of angry feelings often come out.

At first, this happened with Cara, Marianna's daughter, too. But during the time we were there, she came to be much more self-sufficient and independent. One week she didn't want to be in Marianna's group. Sometimes she wanted to sit on Chuck's lap. During the last day, she drew pictures for all of us and spent time around Chuck, Marianna and me individually.

The content, caring, and length of our program gave Cara room to grow like this. It was also really important for Cara to be able to know something about what Marianna's work and interests outside the house are. It's always important for children to have contact with their parents in the workplace. It seems vital to us that young people whose parents are working on issues of empowering children understand what their parents' work is all about.

—Ellen Forsythe

An important aspect of the work I was doing at the Children's School was being with my daughter. A new dimension was added to our relationship. I learned new ways of being with her and her friends. When I sat down at the end of the year to write up my experiences at the school, I asked Cara what was good about my being in her class. She said, "I liked it when someone would say, 'Your Mom's here,' and I'd get so excited that I didn't want to sit down."

—Marianna Cayten

70

FINAL EVALUATION

Editor's Note: *The notes taken at the final evaluation do not include the names of each person, as they do for the mid-term evaluation. Maybe they weren't recorded because everybody was so "high" with excitement, good feelings, and celebration at the final session, which preceded the evaluation. At any rate, what follows is an attempt to make a summary of the evaluation, while keeping people's own words as much as possible.*

What's Been Good About This Year?

Growth in the Children

Hugs this morning. It's a fantastic culmination of the work we've done. Everyone was really affectionate with everyone else.

Nonviolence and Children has really helped to give the kindergartners more skills in saying things they like: verbalizing positive things in their world, encouraging them to say good things at an important time in their life, letting them know that it's OK to say these things, and increasing the number of words they have with which to do so.

The children have grown within our program. They've done things they wouldn't have done without us. Playing "This Is a Hug" this morning is an example.

Growth in Us

The growing that we did at the Children's School was fantastic. Ellen and Marianna both became more self-confident. We had a chance to explore the use of books and puppets in a classroom and to get experience working with younger children. The teachers had a successful session leading groups when we couldn't be there, which indicated that we're passing on skills. It was a supportive environment for us to experiment and grow in.

Ellen got much more relaxed while working here. The tenseness and the worry that was on her face at the beginning of the year has disappeared. Karen and Jessica helped us to learn about verbalizing rules and helping to get the children to follow them. The structure that they set up helped the children to participate—having small groups, dividing the children into those groups with some thought, insisting on their listening, and being firm about expectations.

We got better at not sticking to our plan, but doing what made sense in each group at the time.

We learned some of the limitations of children of that age, and learned once again that children will model our behavior. But we also learned that it was important to be daring and not to follow too closely any set ideas of what children of a certain age can do. It became obvious to us that we can't predict children's reactions and that developmental theories or pictures of children aren't fully accurate. Given confidence, support, love and delight, children can do amazing things.

For the Teachers

Having other adults in the room on a consistent basis gave Karen and Jessica some new perspectives on themselves.

Chuck's presence in the classroom was important for the children. He was the only man who consistently came into the classroom. It was especially important to Daryll and Mitch to have him there.

The five of us communicated well. Karen and Jessica did not feel as if they were on show. We were able to learn some things from them, and they from us. An important thing that we learned was to wait, and to expect children to listen.

Affirmation

The affirmation work we did was especially important. It fit into the class. That week when we affirmed Karen was one of the best.

Puppetry

The span and development of the work with puppets was good; using puppets for affirmation, exploring feelings, and conflict resolution. It has been effective to have a general supply of puppets in the room all the time. The puppet shows were a good way to explore the feelings that were on top, and to think about topics that related to feelings. Previously, we'd thought about puppets just for conflict resolution and for generating many different solutions, but not for exploring feelings.

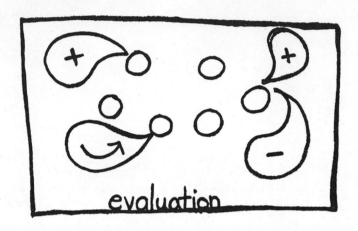

What Could Have Been Changed?

When we introduce our program, we could emphasize more strongly that we are teaching tools to deal with common problems which everyone has. We are not therapists coming to analyze students and we aren't here to try to solve the problems of the emotionally-disturbed children. Karen and Jessica understood this, but others don't so readily.

There is room in our program to use role-playing, taking off on the use of puppets. Jessica used to think that you couldn't do role-plays with really young children, but now she realizes that children role-play all the time. It is one of the ways they have to experiment with different values. We would be structuring the role-play that they do all the time. Perhaps we could do it in three groups and run it through twice.

One idea we never got around to trying was letting the children use mirrors to affirm themselves.

Occasionally, at the end of a session, it would have been good to share what each small group had done. We had trouble, though, coordinating the ending time of the small groups.

The children's attention span grew during the year. It's stilted, therefore, to have a set length of time for a program such as ours. We might try to think of ways to integrate our program into the morning in a more flowing way.

It would have been valuable to have the teachers from different schools where we have worked to get together and share insights with each other about our work and how it is to have the Nonviolence and Children people in the classroom.

We could have done more with the parents. It would have been a good place for a parent support group.

We didn't get to evaluate with Karen and Jessica for the last several weeks because they had parent conferences at our evaluation time.

Editor's Note: *Karen Zaur, who taught with Jessica at the Children's School when the Nonviolence and Children Program was working there, joined the Nonviolence and Children Collective the following year. So we feel that she has a unique perspective to add to this account.*

A Special Time

Early in the weeks that we had the Nonviolence and Children people coming on Tuesdays, a sense began to build in our classroom that we could expect something special on Tuesday mornings. That "something special" was that Marianna and Chuck and Ellen, three big people who cared about the children as a class and as individuals, would be there. It was that there would be lots of good singing and sharing of some sort. Maybe another parent would be there to join one of the three groups, which would be special, too.

This year, while my major work is with the Nonviolence and Children Program, I sometimes substitute at the Children's School. Someone usually remembers that I now do "what Marianna and Ellen and Chuck did last year." I'm usually asked for a song, especially "Do Your Ears Hang Low?" It's the remarks, "Oh, yeah, I remember when they came...why don't they come anymore?...It was nice when they came," and the vibes I get from the children that tell me they know something special was happening at those sessions.

It certainly was special for me, too. It was very exciting to watch people whom I really liked and trusted organize and present a mini-curriculum of all those affective (is it still OK to use that word?) principles which I always believed were at the basis of my teaching.

It was also special that we had three people as models for the children. I always like to think that I can teach a little "vocational education" along the way, even with the youngest children. So it was exciting for me to be able to introduce the Nonviolence and Children people in a way that let the children know that what Chuck, Ellen and Marianna were doing was their "work."

Sitting Back

There are many things which the Nonviolence and Children people did near the end of the year that they probably could not have done so effectively at the beginning. The children needed to get to know them and trust them first. Because I had known and taught many of the children for two and three years, I might have been able to go in one day, for example, and do some conflict resolution activity without the organized build-up which Chuck, Ellen and Marianna did. That, I suppose, is what all this business of applying technique flexibly is about. It's also why our teacher workshops this year have been so effective. Some teachers, once they learn the skills, theory and approaches, can apply them to their own classrooms right away.

However, being able to see conflict resolution and the more difficult activities emerge in the group which Marianna and Chuck and Ellen led was a real treat. I had the unique opportunity to see all over again, and this time with a bit of distance, how various personalities in my class grouped themselves and became a community. Community-building had already happened on some level at the beginning of the year, with lots of wishing and hoping on my part. But I hadn't had a chance just to sit back and watch it.

Given a Class Now

This brings up the question that has been running around in my mind ever since I joined the Nonviolence and Children Program. Given a class right now, would I decide to set a certain part of the day or week aside for such activities in an organized, developmental way? Or would I use the added information and technique as part of my repertoire, hoping to remember the best of it when the time was right?

Probably I would do both. I've been thinking about the various ways I'd approach each goal. For instance, I always worked a lot on community building, especially at the beginning of the year. Of course, much depended on the particular group of children each year, but this is an area I feel good about. It's part of my style. But in the future I'd *talk* with the children about community-building, and about why we do it. We'd talk about the things we might like to do together, and about the things we *can* do *better* together when we feel like "one big happy family."

At the Children's School, we always felt somewhat special because we were so identified with our small, special building. But if I were teaching in a regular school building, I'd follow the example of some friends of mine. They help their classes choose a name ("The Jackson 5's"... "The Yellow Submarine") to help maintain a sense of something special about their particular classroom within a larger school. During the first few weeks of the year, some activities can center on the name which the group has chosen—a sign for the door and decorations for the room.

What's clear to me, after this year, is that I'd think more consciously about particular goals, such as community-building, and I'd talk with the students about "theory" as well as "activities."

With the other goals—affirmation, conflict resolution, sharing feelings—I'd really like to try scheduling a time for them on a regular basis, and in addition do a special project around one of them, such as affirmation silhouettes. I'd like to stay continually aware of how important those goals are in my teaching. That awareness would help to keep the goals closely integrated into my whole style.

Some things get precedence, and not always because the teacher and the children wish it. My wish would be to give precedence to the goals of Nonviolence and Children in much the same way that we give it to the three R's.

Devote a Time

We've talked in the Collective this year about how the things we've been doing should permeate the classroom, so that maybe planning activities on a regular basis isn't so important. But I disagree. There's a lot that permeates a classroom. For instance, language arts really runs through the whole day. Nonetheless, it's still important to devote a particular time to language, to find out where individual children are in their language work, and to give them activities to build their skills. This particular time also makes the children feel confident that they are "actively" learning to read, write, etc.

I think the same is true with our program's goals. Of course they should permeate the day. And in addition, lucky the child who can say that she or he is actively learning to solve problems, share feelings, and affirm others and self.

When the teacher takes time to teach something specific, this says something to the child. If children see a teacher practicing *and* actively teaching affirmation, they will assume that affirmation is an important value and goal. Teaching by modelling isn't to be underestimated—ever.

It's all part of letting children take charge of their own learning. A first step towards this surely is to develop an ability to articulate what one is learning in school and what one wants to learn.

A smart, thoughtful combination of teaching, practicing, and remembering to let the kids in on all the theory, too—that feels right.

Creating an Environment

Editor's Note: *Tom Ewell is a teacher at Cambridge Friends School. Sukie Rice, who attended a Nonviolence and Children workshop, is a staffperson at the Cambridge office of the American Friends Service Committee. Tom's article demonstrates what one or two individuals can begin to do in a school.*

by Tom Ewell

reprinted from Peacework*
April 1976

Last summer I, with the other counsellors at Friends China Camp in Maine, tried to live and apply the philosophy and techniques of affirmative education.

When I returned to school last Fall I was anxious to apply what I had learned during the summer. After a false start with a class that was way too large and unruly, I asked Sukie Rice to join me in another attempt to make it work. We met for 6 weeks on a voluntary basis with a dozen 7th and 8th grade students.

Sukie had already visited the class twice, so we began with her telling the students about some of her memories of being their age. She spoke of always worrying about belonging and having to compete for popularity, grades and prettiness, and not being allowed to "be herself." The quiet in the class suggested recognition of the problem and sympathy. We said we hoped to provide a place where those things weren't so important, where we could enjoy each other and "be ourselves." Then we tried a game of pairing up and talking to each other about things we like doing. We then "introduced" one another using the information from the dialogues. The girls seemed to enjoy the personal attention, but the boys were very uneasy with this verbal, non-physical game. We tried another "talking" game which dissolved into total chaos. We ended the class with a "closing circle" in which everyone had a chance to evaluate the class with thumbs up or thumbs down according to whether they liked different aspects of it. We were disappointed that most everything was a downer.

The second session went better. The kids seemed to know what to expect. They gathered together immediately and didn't hassle over what games would be played. They were also prepared for the "quiet talk" before we began. It was the way we began each session.

We played 3 games that day. First, the "Human Pretzel" where, holding hands, everyone gets into a terrible tangle and has to get unwound. The kids wanted "Adverbs" where qualities get pantomimed and guessed. Finally, we created machines, each person being a part of the human lawnmower or garbage-disposal that was built amid much laughter and cooperation. These games were chosen because we all had a chance to be involved and the success of each game was dependent largely on the participation of everyone. When we called for a closing circle, everyone moved right toward it and even put out their arms to include each other. What a difference from the usual situation! Then we all responded to the request that each say something he or she enjoyed from the day's class. Some students "passed" (a right they *always* had) but most made a definite statement.

Throughout the course we tried to follow a similar program of active, non-active and theater games. Some of the games were suggested by the kids and each session ended in an evaluation by the students which formed the basis of our planning the following week's class. An important note here: Sukie and I agreed to set as a priority to meet each week to evaluate the previous session and to plan carefully the next. This was a crucial agreement as our insistence on it kept us going and, in the long run, was the source of our consistency and flexibility.

Some days were disappointments. Role-plays in which we introduced the concept of trying to resolve potential conflicts didn't work well. But each week the group seemed to get along better together. Enthusiasm was high. The kids seemed to look forward to coming. We played games where inclusion of every child was the highest priority, as exclusion seemed to be a major upset in many of their lives. Certain games were found to be successful exactly because the point of them was to make sure

---

* This article was originally entitled "Teaching Nonviolence—Affirmation in the Classroom."

everyone was included in order for "the group to win." What we felt we were able to do was to provide a lively, mostly non-verbal, exciting environment without its being a place where one had to "perform" in order to get positive attention.

The last 2 sessions were especially rewarding. I was aware of the growing ease toward Sukie and me by the declining need for discipline (despite the class being held at an "itchy" end-of-the-day time), and by the general eagerness to have the class.

At the next to the last session, spirits were high. During the closing circle some spoke of wanting to continue the class the following semester. For the last session we played games the kids most enjoyed and could run themselves. We closed by giving the "affirmation" Christmas cards we made, with notes on what we appreciated about them.

Creating this kind of environment was much more difficult in the hustle and bustle of the school than in the smaller, closer community of the summer camp. I hope that as we get better at this kind of work, perhaps doing more of it in the lower grades where it can be more accepted, we can eventually provide a "critical mass" of influence within the larger community of the school—other students, teachers, parents, administration. At any rate our brief experiment at the Friends School was a successful one, and we recommend attempting some form of it for many kinds of situations.

Magic Meetings

Editor's Note: *Lois Dorn recently joined the Nonviolence and Children staff. Her article demonstrates how some of the approaches of this manual can be applied at home.*

by Lois Dorn

reprinted from Fellowship
October 1975

My son, Gregg, 7, was lying on a pillow, legs waving to and fro above his head. He looked curiously like a calf waiting to be branded. My husband, Fred, gave him a loving pat and encouraged him to sit up and join in.

"We're ready to start the meeting and we need your attention," Fred persuaded. "I'm tired," grumbled Gregg.

I made a mental note to suggest moving up the time of our family meeting next week. With school back in session, we were all getting up earlier now, and a lot of our evening energy was being used on homework.

"How would you all like to learn the new round that I learned this weekend?" I ventured. Gregg popped back up into the circle with a smile. When it comes to singing, you never catch Gregg napping. After a few tentative tries at "Fish and Chips and Vinegar," Kurt, 8, made his inevitable request for "Magic Penny" and everyone joined in energetically: "...Love is something if you give it away, you end up having more..." Even on the grumpiest days, that song seems to make us feel good about being together.

"Any last minute suggestions for the agenda before we get started?" I asked. "Can we have a fire?" Paul, 11, suggested. Although we all agreed that a fire in the fireplace would be a special addition, Fred reminded us that we were getting a late start tonight and it might be best to wait till next week's meeting. "I'll be glad to help with the wood," Paul volunteered. Sharing the responsibility for making our meeting place cheerful, and for cleaning up when we are through, is one of the major ground rules for family meeting day.

"Speaking of fires," our chronic worrier, Kurt, proposed, "can we talk again about emergency fire routes? We haven't practiced them in a long time." The suggestion was a good one, as we have recently installed new storm windows, and I suddenly realized the children might not know how to open them. It was decided that the topic of fire routes should be placed at the top of our list of future agendas.

A quick glance at Gregg found him drooping again. I realized that we had better start moving along. We quickly got through such weighty subjects as Job Reviews and Babysitter Rules, finally arriving at TV Schedules. Kurt began his discourse for more TV. I reflected on how much more positive these discussions have become in recent months.

A year ago, I was acting as a one person censorship board on TV programs. The result was oceans of tears, shed mostly by Kurt, who in his shyness, finds great comfort in TV. Tired of the tears and arguing about the merits of this or that cartoon, I finally pulled the plug on the set; and we spent three blissful (for me, at least) summer months of songfests on the porch and late night story hours with everyone piled into one bed. With the return of cold weather, however, came televised football games, and I was less arbitrary about denying my husband TV than I had been about denying the children. As the current surged back into our set, my relationship with the boys was once again charged with familiar arguments about what did or did not constitute a decent TV show. I kept trying to resolve the situation with reasonable explanations. But clearly, our personal communications system was over-taxed and suffering from a few overloaded fuses.

I'm not sure whether it was a sense of democracy or just the gift of gab that got our original family forums going. When the boys were very little, we began using the dinner table as a place to talk about what everyone was doing. As the boys grew older and their range of activities and responsibilities began to expand, the dinner conversations gradually deteriorated. Instead of happy chatter, we found ourselves caught up in a daily routine of tattling and long-winded discourses on basic moral principles and proper social behavior. Our talk times were getting to be more of a lecture series than a sharing time. The boys generally left the table feeling angry with each other and bored with us. Fred and I were sharing a case of chronic indigestion. It was at a workshop on Nonviolence and Children that I got my first ideas for a new approach to this frustrating situation.

I went to my first meeting with Stephanie Judson prepared for a discussion on "to play or not to play with toy guns." Although the subject did come up briefly, Stephanie made it clear that nonviolence, as the project collective was dealing with it, had a much broader meaning and often much more subtle manifestations than war toys. I left that meeting realizing that our seemingly temperate home was suffering from a very common form of domestic violence...over-verbalization. We were beating our children into the ground with all our talk!

I participated in a week long workshop with Stephanie at Friends General Conference at Ithaca, and later I spent a weekend at a teacher-training workshop given by the Collective at Chamounix Mansion in Philadelphia. In each of these experiences, I found myself tremendously impressed. By setting up a clearly defined structure, agreed upon by the participants, and by playing down the role of those responsible for the flow (facilitators, *not* leaders), the group developed a sense of unity and involvement. Participation was made comfortable through the use of trust building activities: games, singing, and affirmations. Problem solving became a happy occupation. Surely, I felt, I could use these tools at home.

At first, our new family get-togethers were mostly fun and games with a few items for discussion introduced by Fred and me. It didn't take long for the boys to get the idea, and begin to want to add some in-put. A family brainstorming session produced a very simple structure on which to build our meetings. A note board was placed in the kitchen where suggested items for the agenda can be noted ahead of time. Personal or family concerns are listed and even games, new songs, poems or little stories to be shared. On the day before the meeting the facilitators, one parent and one child chosen on a revolving basis, make up the agenda. Activities are varied to keep it fun. Everyone pitches in to prepare a cheerful environment in which to meet. The main

thing is to try to deal with the nuts and bolts end of parenting and being parented without undue strain. We join together as a group to work out problems in a pleasant way.

Occasionally something comes up that obviously deals more with feelings than events. We don't attempt to work these things out in our family meetings. Special time is set aside to talk about what the feelings are and how they can be dealt with. Using a method called Re-evaluation Counseling, we encourage family members to release those feelings and clear the way for new understanding. We keep the purpose of our family meetings to loving problem-solving.

This week's meeting came to a close with everyone feeling satisfied. The TV issue had been "sent to committee." Sunday night had been set aside to choose shows from the weekly TV supplement for consideration. Two people would be assigned to each show to review it. In two weeks we will discuss our evaluations of the shows and attempt to set up a list of programs that fit comfortably with the standards that our family tries to live by. Everyone reported that their share of household chores was going well. Kurt complained that he is getting tired of feeding the two dogs and Paul complained that he is tired of D.D.D. (Dog Dirt Detail). Perhaps next week, when chores are up for their voluntary two week rotation, Paul and Kurt may want to switch ends of the dogs. We closed for the evening with a game called "This Is a Hug," and Gregg led the way cheerfully to bed.

As we are Quakers, the word "meeting" is used often in our home and the context varies. Our children frequently ask, "Are you going to a meeting to work or a meeting to worship?" In our family meetings I think we have combined the meanings. We come together to celebrate our joy in sharing the work of being a family.

Meeting Facilitation*

by Berit Lakey

Meetings are occasions when people come together to get something done, whether it is sharing information or making decisions. They may be good, bad or indifferent. Some of the ingredients of good meetings are:

- commonly understood goals
- a clear process for reaching those goals
- an awareness that people come with their personal preoccupations and feelings as well as an interest in the subject at hand
- a sense of involvement and empowerment (people feeling that the decisions are *their* decisions; that they are able to do what needs doing)

While there is no foolproof way to insure successful meetings, there are a number of guidelines that will go a long way toward helping groups to meet both joyfully and productively. Most people can learn how to facilitate a good meeting, but it does take some time and attention. The more people within a group who are aware of good group process skills, the easier the task of the facilitator and the more satisfactory the meeting.

A facilitator is not quite the same as a leader or a chairperson, but more like a clerk in a Quaker meeting. A facilitator accepts responsibility to help the group accomplish a common task: to move through the agenda in the time available and to make necessary decisions and plans for implementation.

A facilitator makes no decisions for the group, but suggests ways that will help the group to move forward. He or she works in such a way that the people present at the meeting are aware that *they* are in charge, that it is *their* business that is being conducted, and that each person has a role to play.

It is important to emphasize that the responsibility of the facilitator is to *the group* and its work rather than to the individuals within the group. Furthermore, a person with a high stake in the issues discussed will have a more difficult task functioning as a good facilitator.

Agenda Planning

If at all possible, plan the agenda before the meeting. It is easier to modify it later than to start from scratch at the beginning of the meeting. If very few agenda items are known before the meeting starts, try to anticipate by thinking about the people who will be there and what kind of process will be helpful to them.

In the agenda include:

1) Something to **gather** people, to bring their thoughts to the present, to make them recognize each other's presence (singing, silence, brief mention of good things that have happened to people lately, etc.)

2) **Agenda review** It's a good idea to have the agenda written on large sheets of newsprint or on a blackboard, so that everybody can see it. By reviewing the agenda the facilitator can give the participants a chance to modify the proposed agenda and then to contract to carry it out.

* Copies of this article on Meeting Facilitation are available for $.35 apiece from the Religious Education Committee, Philadelphia Yearly Meeting, 1515 Cherry St., Philadelphia, PA 19102.

3) **Main items** If more than one item needs to be dealt with it is important to set priorities:

a. If at all possible, start with something that can be dealt with reasonably easily. This will give the group a sense of accomplishment and energy.

b. The more difficult or lengthier items, or those of most pressing importance, come next. If there are several, plan to have quick breaks between them to restore energy and attention (just a stretch in place, a rousing song, a quick game).

c. A big item may be broken into several issues and discussed one at a time to make it more manageable. Or it may be helpful to suggest a process of presenting the item with background information and clarification, breaking into small groups for idea sharing and making priorities, and then returning to the main group for discussion.

d. Finish with something short and easy to provide a sense of hope for next time.

4) **Announcements**

5) **Evaluation** Serves several purposes: to provide a quick opportunity for people to think through what happened and to express their feelings about the proceedings and thus to provide a sense of closure to the experience; and to learn to have better meetings in the future.

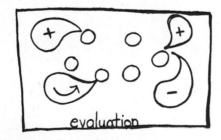

evaluation

Estimate the time needed for each item and put it on the agenda chart. This will:

• indicate to participants the relative weights of the items

• help participants tailor their participation to the time available

• give a sense of the progress of the meeting

Facilitating a Meeting

The tone of the meeting is usually set in the beginning. It's important to start on a note of confidence and energy and with the recognition that those present are people, not just roles and functions. Sometimes singing will do this—especially in large gatherings—or a quick sharing of good things that have happened to individual people lately. The time it takes is repaid by the contribution it makes to a relaxed and upbeat atmosphere where participants are encouraged to be real with each other.

Agenda Review

1) Go through the whole agenda in headline form, giving a brief idea of what is to be covered and how.

2) Briefly explain the rationale behind the order of the proposed agenda.

3) Then, and not before, ask for questions and comments.

4) Don't be defensive of the agenda you have proposed, but don't change everything at the suggestion of one person—check it out with the group first.

5) If major additions are proposed, make the group aware that adjustments must be made because of limited time available, like taking something out, postponing something until later, etc.

6) If an item that some people do not want to deal with is suggested for discussion, consider that there is no consensus and it cannot be included at that time.

7) Remember that your responsibility as facilitator is to the whole group and not to each individual.

8) When the agenda has been amended, ask the participants if they are willing to accept it—and insist on a response. They need to be aware of having made a contract with you about how to proceed. Besides, it is their meeting!

Agenda Items Proper

1) Arrange (before the meeting) to have somebody else present each item.

2) Encourage the expression of various viewpoints—the more important the decision, the more important it is to have all pertinent information (facts, feelings, and opinions) on the table.

3) Expect differences of opinion—when handled well, they can contribute greatly to creative solutions.

4) Be suspicious of agreements reached too easily—test to make sure that people really do agree on essential points.

5) Don't let discussion continue between two people, but ask for comments by others. After all, it is the group that needs to make the decisions and carry them out.

6) As much as possible, hold people to speaking for themselves *only* and to being specific when they refer to others. Do not accept: "*some* people say...," "*we* all know...," "*they* would not listen...." Even though this is scary in the beginning, it will foster building of trust in the long run.

7) Keep looking for minor points of agreement and state them—it helps morale.

8) Encourage people to think of fresh solutions as well as to look for possible compromises.

9) In tense situations or when solutions are hard to reach, remember humor, affirmation, quick games for energy, change of places, small buzz groups, silence, etc.

10) When you test for consensus, state in question form everything that you feel participants agree on. Be specific: "Do we agree that we'll meet on Tuesday evenings for the next two months and that a facilitator will be found at each meeting to function for the next one?" Do NOT merely refer to a previous statement: "Do you all agree that we should do it the way it was just suggested?"

11) Insist on a response. Here again the participants need to be conscious of making a contract with each other.

12) If you find yourself drawn into the discussion in support of a particular position, it would be preferable to step aside as facilitator until the next agenda item. This can be arranged beforehand if you anticipate a conflict of interest.

13) Almost any meeting will benefit from quick breaks in the proceedings—energy injections—provided by short games, songs, a common stretch, etc.

Evaluation

In small meetings (up to 50 people at least) it is often wise to evaluate how things went (the meeting process, that is, not the content). A simple format: on top of a large sheet of newsprint or a blackboard put a $+$ on the left side, a $-$ in the middle, and a $\nearrow$ on the right side. Under the $+$ list positive comments, things that people felt good about. Under the $-$ list the things that could have been done better, that did not come off so well. Under the $\nearrow$, list specific suggestions for how things could have been improved.

Don't get into arguments about whether something was in fact helpful or not; people have a right to their feelings. It is not necessary to work out consensus on what was good and what was not about the meeting.

A few minutes is usually all that is needed—don't drag it out. Try to end with a positive comment.

Meetings almost invariably get better after people get used to evaluating how they function together.

Closing

Try to end the meeting in the same way it started—with a sense of gathering. Don't let it just fizzle. A song, some silence, standing in a circle, shaking hands—anything that affirms the group as such and puts a feeling of closure on the time spent together is good.

"Vibes Watcher"

At times when the discussion is expected to be particularly controversial or when there are more people than the facilitator can be awarely attentive to, it may make sense to appoint a "vibes watcher"—a person who will pay attention to the emotional climate and energy level of the attenders. Such a person is encouraged to interrupt the proceedings when necessary with an observation of how things are going and to suggest remedies when there is a problem.

As "vibes watcher" you pay most attention to the nonverbal communication, such as:

- body language — are people yawning, dozing, sagging, fidgeting, leaving?
- facial expressions — are people alert or "not there," looking upset, staring off into space?
- side conversations — are they distracting to the facilitator or to the group?
- people interrupting each other.

It is often difficult to interpret such behavior correctly. Therefore, it may be wise to report what you have observed and possibly suggest something to do about it. If energy is low a quick game, a stretch, or a rousing song may wake people up. If tension or conflict level is preventing people from hearing each other, getting up and finding new places to sit may help. A period of silence may also be helpful, in which people can have a chance to relax a bit and look for new insights.

It is important for the vibes watcher to keep a light touch and not make people feel guilty or defensive. Also, be confident in your role; there is no reason for apologizing when you have an observation or a suggestion for the group—you are doing them a favor.

Process Observer

From time to time any group can benefit from having somebody observe how it works. During periods of conflict or transition (changing consciousness about sexism, for example) a process observer may be of special value.

While functioning as a process observer, be careful not to get involved in the task of the group. A notepad for short notations will help you to be accurate. Remember to notice helpful suggestions or procedures that moved the group forward. Once a group has a sense of its strengths, it is easier to consider the need for improvements.

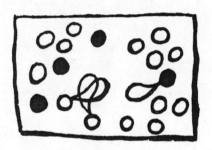

Here are *some* specific things you might look for:

- What was the general atmosphere in which the group worked? (relaxed, tense)
- How were the decisions made?
- If there was any conflict, how was it handled?
- Did everybody participate? Were there procedures that encouraged participation?
- How well did the group members listen to each other?
- Were there recognized leaders within the group?
- How did the group interact with the facilitator?
- Were there differences between male and female participation?

82

When you as process observer (whether appointed or not) are paying specific attention to patterns of participation, an easy device would be to keep score on paper. In a small group a mark can be made next to a person's name every time she or he speaks. If you are looking for differences in participation patterns between categories of people, such as male-female, black-white, new member-old member, keeping track of number of contributions in each category is enough.

In giving feedback to the group, try to be matter-of-fact and specific so that people do not get defensive and can know exactly what you are talking about. Again, remember to mention the strengths you observed in the group.

If you take it upon yourself to function as a process observer without checking it with the group beforehand, be prepared for some hostility. Your contribution may turn out to be very valuable, but much tact and sensitivity is called for.

Co-facilitator

Instead of the usual practice of having one facilitator, it is often wise to have two. Here are some of the reasons and circumstances for team facilitation:

1) More information and ideas are available during the planning.

2) More energy (physical and emotional) is available to the group, especially during times of conflict or when handling complicated matters.

3) If a facilitator becomes personally involved in the discussion, it is easy to hand the job over to the co-facilitator for the time being.

4) Co-facilitation is a way for more people to gain experience and become skilled facilitators.

5) It is less exhausting demanding, and scary.

For people who are not used to working as a team it is probably wise to divide responsibility for the agenda clearly before the meeting. However, co-facilitation means that the person who is currently not "on duty" is still responsible for paying attention as "vibes watcher" and pitching in to help clarify issues, test for consensus, and so on.

In evaluating their work together, people who work as co-facilitators can help each other by giving feedback and support, and thus learn and grow.

Staffings

Staffings, or staff reviews, are regular meetings in which teachers work together to take a concentrated look at the school histories of individual students and to focus on particular issues or concerns about their students.* Each teacher has a turn to be the "referring teacher" who "presents" a child to the group by describing the student at some length and putting forth a problem or concern. The presentation requires observation and preparation ahead of time, which are often helpful in themselves. The staff review meeting provides an opportunity for teachers to work together creatively to share insights and support and to build a sense of community among themselves.

As a teacher at Powel School, a public elementary school in the School District of Philadelphia, Karen Zaur participated in staffings.** Then, from November through June, 1975-76, as part of her work with the Nonviolence and Children Program, she served as a consultant on staffings to teachers at Lea and Durham Schools, two other public schools in Philadelphia. This is Karen's account of the staffing process.

A Few Words About What Follows

At Powel School, then at Lea and Durham, I found that each teacher group evolved its own style of staffing. Each group made some alterations in the Format for Staff Review from the Prospect School. While the following format is my synthesis of the best changes and adaptations made by the groups I have worked with, it retains the basic Prospect outline.

—*Karen Zaur*

---

* The staff review process originated from the staff of the Prospect School in North Bennington, Vermont. Under the direction of Patricia Carini, the Prospect School staff is studying ways to document a child's school history and to use that information in fostering the child's development, in organizing curricula, and so forth.

** Staff members at several public schools in Philadelphia, through their relationship with the Advisory Center of the School District of Philadelphia and the Prospect School, have adapted and implemented staff reviews on a weekly basis.

Outline of Staff Review Format

I. Excitement-sharing

II. Chairperson opens the meeting

III. Referring teacher "presents" the student

IV. Chairperson summarizes important points of presentation

V. Other group members give additional pertinent input

VI. Chairperson summarizes new information

VII. Group members ask clarifying questions; chairperson mediates questions and summarizes new information

VIII. Group makes recommendations to referring teacher

IX. Recorder reads list of recommendations

X. Participants evaluate the session

XI. Closing the meeting/filing information

Rotating Responsibilities and Roles

Chairperson   Evaluation person

Recorder   Snack person

Referring teacher

Annotated Staff Review Format

I. Excitement-sharing

Each member of the group takes a minute or two to tell of something pleasant that has happened lately or something that will happen in the near future. This kind of personal sharing starts the meeting off on a positive note, away from the day's distractions. It also sets a precedent for everyone to participate in the proceedings, although the right to pass should be maintained. Try sharing small pleasures as well as major events. Excitement-sharing helps to build a sense of community in the group.

II. Chairperson Opens the Meeting

The chairperson opens by:

A. Checking that the recorder and evaluator for this meeting are prepared and that everything is ready.

B. Introducing the referring teacher, giving the name and age of the student to be presented and, in a few words, describing the problem or issue about which the referring teacher is concerned.

III. Referring Teacher "Presents" the Student

This includes the following information:

A. Statistical data

 1. Name

 2. Age

 3. Length of stay in this school

B. Presenting the problem (concisely)

 The particular area of concern which the referring teacher would like the group to focus on during the staff review.

85

C. Profile
1. Physical development and coordination
2. Social development and relationships
3. Emotional development (including ways of expressing anger)
4. Academic performance
5. Interests and facility for involvement
6. Strengths

D. Additional commentary, and examples of the child's work: drawings, writings, etc.

IV. Chairperson Summarizes Important Points of Presentation

The chairperson summarizes information here and in steps VI and VII.

A summary includes a brief synopsis of the information, highlighting the most important points and themes. It isn't necessary or helpful to repeat all the information which has been presented.

The chairperson's role is flexible. Sometimes summaries aren't needed at these particular times. Sometimes they seem appropriate to clarify things during the presentation or the questions.

V. Other Group Members Give Additional Pertinent Input

Now it is particularly helpful to hear from teachers who have known the child in previous years. This fosters a longitudinal view of the student.

VI. Chairperson Summarizes New Information

See step IV.

VII. Group Members Ask Clarifying Questions; Chairperson Mediates Questions and Summarizes New Information

Thoughtful questions from members of the group will lead to good recommendations in step VIII. It is important to keep the referring teacher's problems or issues about the particular student in mind when formulating questions.

See step IV for summaries from chairperson.

VIII. Group Makes Recommendations to Referring Teacher

Trusted colleagues are an important resource. Almost every recommendation has the potential to spark the referring teacher to thoughtful action. Even if the recommendation is only a little different from one already given, it should be offered.

It's important that the referring teacher not discuss or respond to any recommendations while they're being given. This might close off other recommendations. This is the time to collect ideas which the referring teacher can sort out in the search for what will work best in her or his own situation with the student.

IX. Recorder Reads List of Recommendations

This often sparks a few more ideas, which can be added to the list.

X. Participants Evaluate the Session

The Prospect School suggests a fairly involved critique which analyzes the performance of the chairperson, the referring teacher, and the other participants. Here is a modified version of this critique.

One member of the group briefly summarizes what was good and what might have been better about the chairing of the meeting, the presentation of the student, and the participation of the group as a whole in giving extra information, asking good questions, and offering recommendations. At each meeting a different person takes a turn summarizing.

Lea and Durham teachers used neither of the above. At Lea School, the group decided to go around the table, giving each person a chance to comment positively and negatively on that day's staffing. The Durham teachers adopted the group evaluation format used frequently by the Nonviolence and Children Program (see p.81).

XI. Closing the Meeting/Filing Information

It is important that the group members decide how they will save the recorded minutes of the meeting and how they will keep track of the schedule. A notebook that can be passed around at meetings is useful. One page can easily be a calendar-schedule for the staffings.

86

Roles and Responsibilities To Be Rotated

Among the Group

Chairperson Some of the aspects of the chairperson's role are discussed above. One of her or his main responsibilities is to keep things moving so that everything gets accomplished and the meeting can end on time. Each person will evolve his or her own sense of chairing a staffing. Participants, as well as the chairperson, take responsibility for the meeting, by saving their questions and comments for the appropriate time, by avoiding the temptation to move the conversation away from the topic, and by appreciating the chairperson in the job she or he is doing.

Recorder It is up to the group to decide what will be recorded. Teachers often prepare detailed typed or written presentations which can easily be put in the group's notebook. In that case the recorder might jot down extra information and recommendations only. Referring teachers like to make their own copy of the recommendations to take with them.

Referring Teacher The referring teacher chooses whom to present and prepares the presentation prior to the meeting. (See outline of the presentation in step III above.)

Every child will benefit in his or her school experience from the kind of special attention which a teacher pays to the student being presented for staff review. At the beginning of the school year, teachers often present children who are having a particularly difficult time in one or more areas. However, staffing gives teachers an opportunity to enhance the school experience of many children, not just to get some new ways to deal with a problem. Depending on the frequency of meetings and the size of the group, teachers will have a chance to present a variety of children during the school year.

Evaluation Person (See Evaluation, step X.) The group decides how it wants to evaluate its meetings. If it decides that one person is to do a critique at the end of the meeting, evaluation becomes a separate job to be rotated among the participants. If a group evaluation is used, the chairperson leads one before closing the meeting. The group may decide to experiment with different methods before settling on one.

Snack Person Many staffing groups have established a tradition that the referring teacher provides a light snack for the group.

A Few More Notes About Staffings

Group Size and Frequency of Meetings Group size depends first, of course, on the number of teachers who want to be in the group. A comfortable maximum for a group seems to be seven. If there are more than seven who want to be included, it is good to think about starting a second group.

Many staffing groups meet once a week. This is important at least in the beginning. Weekly meetings establish a momentum in the group, assure time for schedule details and other business to be worked out, and provide a chance for everyone to have a turn presenting a child and chairing a meeting as soon as possible.

After meeting weekly for a while, the teachers at both Lea and Durham decided to meet every other week, leaving more time for other commitments.

Time Ninety minutes should be set aside for the full meeting. The staff review itself should take just over an hour, In addition, there's time spent sharing excitements, scheduling, and taking care of other business details. The first few meetings are likely to be longer than the others, as people spend time clarifying their roles and familiarizing themselves with the process.

Confidentiality Some of the information which is shared by teachers at a staff review session is confidential. A ground rule adopted from the Prospect School is that teachers present no information which is hearsay or gossip. This also applies to things which faculty members know about children and their families outside of the school context. Teachers are asked to present only the information which has been given officially to the school and to them in their capacity as teachers.

Outside Observations Teachers often wish they could step onto the sidelines, unseen, and look at what is "really" happening for a particular child or in a particular area of the room. An outside observer can do that. The observer may be a teacher with a free period, a student teacher, a trusted volunteer, or another outside resource person. Marta Harrison and I did several observations for teachers at Lea and Durham.

An outside observer may spend one or more hours doing an observation, trying to write down absolutely everything which he or she sees and hears. Then the observer goes directly to a typewriter to transcribe the jottings. The typed version can be duplicated and passed out at the staffing.

The observer should be as objective as possible, looking at *what* is happening and *how* it is happening, rather than *why*. It is useful to catch snatches of conversation. In classrooms which are used to having visitors, it is relatively easy to sit on the sidelines and write.

Careful observations of a child are a good source of information for the referring teacher. They also help to round out a picture of the student for others in the staffing group.

Comments on Observations

"I got to hear myself, and the secret language of the classroom."

"...insight into who children spend time with, where they spend choice time..."

"...getting a picture of a child I didn't know..."

"Being observed objectively and having children observed objectively is invaluable. It is so difficult to get a real perception when submerged in the situation."

"...helped me see what a child does on his or her own when I'm not around...other positive strengths and abilities that the child has..."

—*Some Lea and Durham teachers*

"My understanding of the child has changed..."

Time and again, as teachers come to present a child, they remark that their understanding of the child has changed in the short time they have been paying attention to him or her in order to prepare a presentation. For instance, after one staffing I had a chance to talk informally with the referring teacher and to compliment her presentation.

"You know," she answered me, "by the time I finished preparing that presentation on Yolanda, I didn't need to do the staffing. I have to respect the style Yolanda is using to deal with her shyness. Just look at all the friends she had this year! She really is developing just fine. And I see that more clearly every time I watch her."

Wow, I thought, that captures a lot of my good feelings about staffing! The teacher's careful preparation and observation had put the problem into perspective.

Wouldn't it be great if we, as teachers, could pay that kind of close attention to every child? Staffing seems to be one way that it can happen for several children each school year.

—*Karen Zaur*

Teacher Support

The teachers I've worked with have seen staffing as a supportive experience. I've been reading evaluations from Lea and Durham teachers with an eye out for specific supportive elements. High on the list is "a regular focused time to meet with co-workers." That regular meeting time can be an opportunity for a variety of concerns and experiences to be explored.

The Lea teachers, for example, after several months of meeting weekly for staff review, decided to alternate staffing with other issues they wanted to share: educational philosophies, finding classroom assistants, biographies, curriculum planning, ideas for next year, etc. The group from each school planned a delicious dinner near the end of the school year. "The time we've spent together could be even better," said one teacher, "if there were *more* time available, *more* staffing dinners, better ways to deal with issues as well as with children."

Throughout the year there was a growing sense of professional and personal appreciation among members of the groups. I see caring and being cared about as a particularly important element of support. One teacher valued getting together as equals, hearing how others approach a similar problem, and being impressed with the variety of alternative recommendations forthcoming. Another teacher felt support involved being able to express problems with a child in a supportive atmosphere, getting good suggestions, and feeling cared about. The teacher who wrote, "I always come away feeling so positive about the child," showed how the caring developed in the group extended itself to the children.

An important aspect of appreciation is self-appreciation. As one teacher said, "I have been validating my own observations and perceptions of a child and/or problem."

—*Karen Zaur*

Parent Support Groups*

by Lois Dorn

and

Anne G. Toensmeier

* A shorter account of parent support groups appeared in an article by Stephanie Judson entitled "Nonviolence Begins at Home," *Fellowship,* October 1975. Reprints (30 cents) are available from Friends Peace Committee, 1515 Cherry St., Philadelphia, PA 19102.

Why Parent Support?

Parents are usually the most influential adults in their children's lives. However, in their efforts to create a good home environment, parents often receive little support. Sexual discrimination against women, poverty, and the isolation of the nuclear family may combine to make parents feel alone and powerless. Negative forces in parents' lives spiral down through generations, as do patterns of behavior. ("I sounded just like my mother when I yelled at my child.") These kinds of forces and feelings can cause destructiveness, or violence.

Parent support groups are one good way to counteract those negative forces. In addition to work in schools and with teachers, the Nonviolence and Children Program has begun to emphasize work with families and with parent support groups.

Support groups form around many common interests; women's and men's support groups, for example, have emerged everywhere in recent years. Support groups are based on the knowledge that within each member is the ability to solve personal problems, particularly when surrounded by a caring, thinking community. Here are peers who will add their own creativity, experience, and perspective to a problem. Here it is safe to talk and listen, to think and experiment, to laugh and perhaps cry. Nurturing peers are especially important when adults are spending most of their days and nights nurturing children and receiving little or no care themselves.

This supportive approach creates an atmosphere which nurtures an individual's ability to work creatively on problems. Being appreciated and affirmed, whether at home, in a meeting, or in a classroom, encourages people to discuss problems openly; it also provides an empowering sense that the problems *can* be solved without permanent physical or emotional damage to anybody involved in the conflict. When parents have an opportunity to draw on this nonviolent atmosphere themselves, they are far more likely to create and model it for their children.

A Pilot Group

Our first parent support group was unique in its origin and spirit. Eight or ten of us had been meeting for several years as the Nonviolence and Children Subcommittee of Friends Peace Committee, helping to think about the program and to support the staff. When it was time for the program to widen its focus from schools to include families, we suddenly looked around the table and discovered that most of us were parents. We agreed to become a pilot parent support group, with Stephanie Judson as facilitator. The change was truly a transformation into a community of support. We looked forward to our monthly meetings as times of renewal, of feeling good about ourselves as parents and as persons. This is what parent support is really all about.

Subjects for our evenings ranged from affirmation in the family to dealing with death and dying. The format of most evenings was similar. We'd begin with "excitement-sharing." Each person took a turn to recount briefly something pleasant—small or significant—in his or her life since we last met. Then we divided into pairs to share childhood experiences related to the evening's theme. ("What games did you enjoy as a child?" "How did you react to competition?" "How was conflict approached in your own family when you were growing up?" "What influence has this had on your own thinking about conflict now?")

When we gathered again as a whole group, anyone was welcome to share insights gained from recalling the past and how it relates to the present. Stephanie would usually follow with a five to ten minute "mini-rap" of thoughts and theories on the evening's theme, developed from the program's work in schools. The rest of the evening was devoted to discussion and action: playing cooperative games, making affirmation notes out of scrap material, role-playing conflicts with puppets and, always, sharing personal experiences, thoughts, questions, and insights.

91

At the end of each evening there was an evaluation. What was good about the meeting? What did we learn? What needs to be changed about our time together? Any suggestions for ways to change?

Since then several of us have established new parent support groups, returning to the original one for support in doing so. Once the authors of this chapter, frustrated by some difficulties in our new group, asked members of the original one for their thinking and were amazed at their insight and our new effectiveness.

More To Learn

There is still a great deal to learn about parent support groups. Our next step is a study group where we are exploring different bodies of knowledge; e.g., parenting theories, the role of the family in American society. We are acting as well as studying, doing such things as writing, public speaking, and giving intergenerational workshops.

Eventually, a whole manual for parent support groups will be possible. In the meantime, we can share here what we have found important.

Finding Members for a Parent Support Group

Each of the parent support groups to date has developed from a different base. Wherever parents share a common interest in childrearing, the possibility is there: a church group, interfaith organization, PTA or school administration might be a starting point. In Abington Quarter, (a group of ten Quaker meetings) we offered a "one-shot," afternoon parent support workshop at a special weekend and later contacted interested participants (see p. 96). Personal contact has been most effective in gathering members and is a good way to find and encourage people who can make the most positive contribution to a group. Fathers, expecially, need to be welcomed. Also welcome are non-parents, who can offer a very special kind of support to parents and to children.

Facilitation

Good, egalitarian process is as important in parent support groups as in other meetings. (See Meeting Facilitation, p. 79.) The facilitator presents a timed agenda for the group to agree to or alter. This kind of agenda for each session is like a roadmap—it makes planning much simpler. Using the same format each time will give confidence to those who co-lead a session. Posting the agenda and asking the group's consent allows people to voice suggestions and concerns while there is still time to make adjustments. Agreed-upon times for each agenda item will make it easier for people to concentrate on the subject instead of wondering if they'll be home on time, and to spread their energy throughout the meeting.

The facilitator helps members to feel safe and comfortable by seeing that there is no interrupting, no commenting in response to sharing, and a clearly understood freedom to pass. (See Sharing, p. 20.) Excitement-sharing (see Affirmation, p. 6) and Attention-Out Activities (see Games, p. G-20) inject fresh energy. Parents' involvement in future planning, and an evaluation by the group, are very important.

It is essential for the facilitator to explain the reasons along the way for each step of the agenda. "Excitement-sharing gives us each a chance to put aside the hassles of the day and to think of some bright spot. That way everyone can be more positive and alert." One of the reasons for explaining each step is the expectation that members will become increasingly responsible about participation in the group. Each may help with planning the evening, and each is capable of facilitating.

However, it is also important to have one or two ongoing facilitators who can think about the needs of the individuals and of the group during and between meetings. For example, when one of us had a concern about children rejecting our nonviolent values, Stephanie found and mailed her an encouraging article comparing backgrounds of Green Berets and conscientious objectors.* If a member has some special distress—a sick child or a painful conflict—the facilitator may arrange for members to phone him or her occasionally. Of course, when members give and take support between meetings, the group can really become a community.

The role of the facilitator is more complex than sticking to an agenda or timing a session. The facilitator should be aware and loving, firm about principle and theory, and flexible about approach. If a group doesn't respond to one method of problem-solving, such as goal-wish problem-solving (see Conflict Resolution, p. 44), the facilitator should consider another approach. Perhaps brainstorming would be just as effective in helping the group to work together in solving a problem. The facilitator who remains thinking, caring and confident will inspire group members to be the same. Facilitators need sensitive support from the group.

Cornerstone of the Group

I see the spirit of affirmation, including self-affirmation, as the cornerstone of every parent support group meeting. It is wonderful, if at first awkward, to state honestly the things we are doing very well. The facilitator can begin this process by carefully restating the ground rules (no questions, reactions, etc.) and then asking each person in the group to tell briefly something that he or she, as a parent or friend to children, handled well this week.

Of course, we have anxieties and real problems, and within a context of affirmation, the feelings about them will undoubtedly come even more to the fore. I remember, on one occasion, a woman in the group was dealing with a crisis. Stephanie set aside a special time for her to share with us what was happening in her life, and then everyone had a chance to tell her what we especially appreciated about her. All of us came away feeling renewed.

When Marta Harrison was about to move away to England, we devoted an entire evening to appreciating her and her contributions to the group. We wrote affirmations on a poster, and even created and "gave" her a personalized game and a song. (See Games, p. G-23, "Catch a Falling Star.")

—*Anne G. Toensmeier*

---

* Mantell, David, "Guess Who Had the Authoritarian Parents," *Psychology Today,* Vol. VIII, No. 4, September 1974, pp. 56-62.

Quest for Answers

If there is one common element among members of support groups, it is their quest for answers. It is important that the facilitator communicate clearly that each person has his or her own best answer. By demonstrating and encouraging the group to try some skills in solving problems, it is possible to help people move past the feeling that "I don't know what to do." Through brainstorming, "how-to" problem-solving, puppetry and role-playing, they will get a sense of their own creative ability to deal with conflict. Trying on new roles and attitudes in the guise of a puppet may bring new insights or a lighter look at an old problem. The activities themselves and the ideas they generate all can be used in the family context as well. Each individual is the best judge of how to adapt them to his or her own needs. As one wise person put it, "Support is me encouraging others to see their own strengths and abilities."

The Roaring Demons Parents' Collective

I am not a natural at parenting; I wasn't one of those young ladies groomed for motherhood from the age of six. I'm beginning to find out that maybe there wasn't any adequate training for what I am now experiencing anyway. Our three children—one of whom we adopted when he was six—are rugged individuals. No one system or theory of child-rearing fits all of them, my husband and me.

If I have any basic approach, it would have to be called the "eclectic theory of child-rearing." I've read my share of child psychologists; I've had Parent Effectiveness Training; and I've taken an Affective Education class for parents. What I've come up with is a system like ordering Chinese take-out; one from Column A and one from Column B. Because of this approach, a large part of my most useful information, insights, and ideas come from sharing experiences with other parents, precisely what our parent support group provided.

Most of the parents in our support group already knew each other. We had patterns of discussing everything from urban renewal to hobbies; we needed direction. Beyond this, I was gratified that the emphasis in our group was as much on the quality of survival of us as *parents* as it was on enriching our children's environment. I think that in the urgency of trying to rear a generation of happy, well-adjusted children, parents often feel reduced to the status of mere provider of experiences, educational toys and field trips.

My evenings spent with other parents who share those frustrations, and still retain some sense of sanity and personal integrity, were a comfort and an active kind of encouragement. I always know somewhere in the back of my head—but it never hurts to be reminded—that I'm not the only one in the world whose normally co-operative six year old becomes a roaring demon when the word "bath" is uttered. I know that others can also end up in the curious position of swatting a ten year old in order to emphasize that hitting doesn't solve anything.

Each of us had valuable insights that were useful to others in the group in coping with their particular hassles and concerns as parents. Somebody else's problems always look clearer, and workable solutions or options appeared joyfully, as though out of the atmosphere, in the goal-wish problem-solving process we used.

The format of a group setting was what I needed to feel really at home with family-centered discussions and problem-solving. As neighbors and now closer friends, we're continuing the group this fall.

—*Maggie Morris*
adapted from Fellowship
October 1975

94

Effecting Change

Parent support groups can be a touchstone to further action. The foundation of a caring community can inspire and sustain adults in their efforts at organizing, political pressure, writing, public speaking, etc., to effect change for themselves and for children. Already-established groups involved in working for change can also find sustenance through the activities and approaches described here and throughout the manual. Where to start, which activities to use, and when, depend on courage and good common sense in the particular situation.

Making It Go

Deciding on topics of discussion is one of the first ways the group can begin to take responsibility for itself. Using part of the first session to brainstorm areas of interest, and then to agree which areas to focus on, will help clarify the direction the group will take. This will also give people a chance to think ahead about resources they would like to see used and ways in which they personally could contribute. Once the group has defined where it wants to go, the facilitators can concentrate on the business of helping it get there.

Although concerns will vary greatly from one group to another, there are some common areas of experience that a group can utilize to achieve a sense of supportiveness. Activities centered around affirmation, sharing feelings, community building, and solving problems will help develop an atmosphere where people reach out thoughtfully to others in the group. A careful reading of the rest of this manual will be helpful to those interested in starting a parent support group.

A Board Meeting

We board members of our alternative elementary school were having a predictably long and tiring meeting about finances. After a couple of hours, I proposed that we play a cooperative game, Musical Laps. Eager for a diversion, people agreed, though dubiously.

We had a great time playing it! Then, somehow, we were fresh to think again about the difficult money questions. We resolved them, and with better spirits.

—*Francy Williams*

One Example

Editor's Note: *During 1975-76, Lois Dorn and Anne Toensmeier facilitated a parent support group for Quakers in Abington Quarter, a geographic area near Philadelphia which includes ten Quaker meetings. The initial recruiting letter, and the agendas, evaluations, and brainstorm lists from three sessions are presented here. We include them, not as a blueprint, but to provide a general idea of what happened in one particular parent support group.*

October 30, 1975

Dear Friends,

At Abington Quarterly Weekend in September a group of Friends took part in a Parent Support Workshop. There we shared experiences and goals, explored common problems, and supported each other in the challenging task of parenting.

With that meeting as a sample, some of us in the Quarter would like to form a Parent Support Group. Our purpose would be to develop a sense of community in which parents could support each other, appreciate each other, and deal with problems as a group. Here we could share ways of incorporating into family life some of the new awarenesses developed by the Nonviolence and Children program.

Topics for meetings, as well as place, time, and frequency of meetings, would depend on the group's choice. One parent support group, though, has dealt with these topics: building community in the family, affirmation, cooperative games, conflict resolution, shared feelings, sex roles, problem solving through synergics.

We are willing to facilitate meetings, drawing on experience in another such parent support group, but we would hope to use group sharing, role-playing, games, and other such techniques as well as discussion to involve everyone.

Our first meeting will be on Thursday, November 20, at 7:30 p.m. at Gwynedd Meeting Schoolhouse. At that time the group will choose future dates and places of meetings as well as topics. Please feel free to phone meanwhile if you have questions or suggestions.

In peace,
Anne G. Toensmeier
Lois Dorn

SESSION 1

Family Appreciation

November 20

Introduction Game

"My name is _____ and I'm good at _____."
(adaption of "Itch Game")

Excitement-sharing

Agenda Review

What's a Parent Support Group?

Description from Anne and Lois
Questions

Sharing in Pairs

"A time when somebody really appreciated me..."

Sharing Insights with Whole Group

Mini-rap

Theory of put-downs and affirmation

Cooperative Game

Elephant-Palm Tree

Puppetry

Sock puppet examples of put-downs

Brainstorming

Ways to appreciate family

Appreciation Cards

Making a card for a family member you want to affirm

Evaluation and Closing

96

BRAINSTORM LIST:
Ways to Appreciate Family

- Love notes
- Lunch box notes
- Special lunch treats
- Special book from the library
- Hug - touch
- Verbal reassurance
- Special gesture
- Drawing a picture
- Blank book—write special appreciation of person

- Remembering what people say/do/like
- Allowing privacy
- Having a special time together
- Responsibility of looking good
- Making someone's life a little easier
- Compliments
- Knowing what someone would like to have appreciated

EVALUATION OF SESSION 1

+ (Good Things)	— (Things That Weren't Good and/or Need Changing)	↗ (Ways to Improve, or Things to Keep in Mind)
Sharing	Meeting too long ⟶	Shorter Agenda
Enthusiasm		
Cake		
Desire to learn from each other	Difficult to get here on time ⟶	Meet later
Warmth		
Unity		
Willingness to participate		Name tags
Entertainment		
		Bring pillow

SESSION 4
Anger

April 19

Excitement-sharing

Agenda Review

Planning Ahead

> Choosing date for next meeting
> Who will plan with Lois for next time?
> Food?
> Summer—shall we meet?
> Who will plan with Anne for Gwynedd program
> May 10?*
> Membership—Do we want to ask others to join
> us?

Sharing in Circle

> What gets you angriest? What successes have
> you had with anger?

Children's Anger: Active-Listening (from Parent
Effectiveness Training)

> Mini-rap and demonstration
> Try it in pairs
> Responses

Cooperative Game

Parents' Anger: I-Statements (from Parent Effectiveness Training)

> Mini-rap
> Discussion

Non-destructive Ways To Get Out Anger

> Brainstorm
> Discussion

Evaluation and Closing

---

* Anne asked that somebody help her present the idea of parent support groups to a mother's group
which asked her to talk with them.

98

BRAINSTORM LIST:
Non-destructive Ways To Get Out Anger

- Place/objects set aside for pounding, throwing, etc.
- Sports
- Something to punch
- Shadow boxing
- Safe place for shouting, etc.
- Needs witness
- Co-counseling
- Pounding pillows
- Work
- Running
- Being outside—give children garden
- Angry pictures
- Clay, sandbox
- Aggressive bread-making

EVALUATION OF SESSION 4

+ *(Good Things)*	— *(Things That Weren't Good and/or Need Changing)*	↗ *(Ways to Improve, or Things to Keep in Mind)*
Ended on time Discussion Open input Well-planned Structure Hugging Close, small Good subject	Need to think ahead——→ Didn't deal with specific prob-——→ lems	Choose next topic ahead of time so group can prepare Time in each meeting for frustration sharing/problem-solving Reminder calls about meeting during month Meet more often Plymouth next time More freedom to pass

SESSION 5
Alternate Christmas Celebration

May 25

Excitement-sharing

Agenda Review

Mini-rap on Holiday Sharing

Cooperative Game

Small Group Sharing

Open Discussion in Whole Group

Cooperative Game
> Pretzel

Brainstorm
> Meaningful changes in your Christmas

Evaluation

Closing

BRAINSTORM LIST:
Meaningful Changes in Your Christmas

- See more of friends than relatives
- Add spirituality to Christmas
- Affirmation of friends and family
- Summer workshop for crafts (with kids)
- Doing something special each day of holiday season
- Special day or something after Christmas
- Family participation in planning
- Helping to get relatives responsive to alternate celebrations
- Send Alternate Celebration Catalogue as a present
- Wean gradually
- Expand Christmas
- Adults exchange stockings
- Exchange gift ideas

EVALUATION OF SESSION 5

+ (Good Things)	— (Things That Weren't Good and/or Need Changing)	↗ (Ways to Improve, or Things to Keep in Mind)
Men at the meeting Great suggestions Positive, creative ideas Sally's cookies Games were fun Prior thinking Not threatening Size of group	Cold Missed Frank and Ellen	Have more information ahead of time about topic

Beginning in 1976, the Nonviolence and Children Program has begun to focus much of its energies on parent and family work. Parent support groups are an important element in this work. We would very much like to know about experiences which others have had with parent support groups. Do let us hear from you!

Books for Young People

A good children's book is a joy for all ages. It touches simply on complex human themes, delights the imagination, and draws us back to read it again and again.

The Nonviolence and Children Program has been collecting such children's books for over two years. We have looked especially for books which fall into three categories encompassing major elements of our understandings about nonviolence.

Conflict Resolution: books that portray people finding creative solutions to conflict

Sex Roles: books about people who are breaking free of rigid cultural sex roles

Feelings: books in which people understand their feelings and deal with them well

Most of the books gathered for these categories are recently-published or not well-known. A few are old favorites. We were excited to discover the little-known ones, and decided to include an annotated booklist in this manual in order to share the information.

Each of the recently-published or lesser-known books is listed under one of the categories above, though several actually fall into more than one category.

This section also includes a list of "old favorite" books which fit into one or more of the three categories, a list of outstanding authors whose books are almost always excellent, and a list of places to write for current and continuing information about new books.

The focus of this bibliography is on books for elementary school age people. The majority are easy readers and picture books which can be read aloud in a single period in a classroom, or in a single sitting at home. If you know of other good children's books such as these, please share them with us.

Using Books in Groups

Reading books aloud is one method of exploring subjects which are important to children. Different books lend themselves to different reading approaches.

For example, *Grownups Cry Too,* by Nancy Hazen, has a complete thought on each page, expressed in a few words. This book inevitably brings up feelings and experiences that children relate to strongly. Therefore, it is best to read this book in a small group, presenting it in such a way that the children see the pictures as the book is read, and to stop at the end of each page to allow children to share their own experiences.

Some books do not lend themselves to stopping at the end of each page for discussion. In such cases, sharing circles (see Sharing, p.23) are helpful for expressing feelings at the end of the story.

102

Sometimes it is necessary to work in large groups. In this situation you may want to read the story first, and to show the picture after each page or at the end of the book. You can follow the reading by breaking into small groups to explore thoughts and feelings related to the book.

You can tell a story yourself after reading a book thoroughly. Use different voices for each character, and encourage the children to act along with you, using their bodies or puppets to do so.

Acting out a whole story by themselves is often too large a task for young children. A small, easy-to-act-out part of a longer story is suitable here. Several children can act out each part, and everybody who wants to can have a turn.

Many stories lend themselves to being adapted into puppet shows. *Tears of the Dragon*, by Hirusuke Hamanda, is a good example of a book on conflict resolution which becomes a superb puppet show. Children and adults together can become totally involved in the story as they present it through puppets.

Many books which are useful for exploring conflict and feelings unfortunately also portray stereotyped sex roles. You can change this through your own comments. For example, *The Quarreling Book* involves a traditional family in which the father goes off to work and the mother stays at home. You might introduce the book by saying, "Many of you probably have families that are different from this one. Some of you may have families that are similar. But most of us have probably had some of the same feelings that people in this story have."

Discovering Children's Books

Part of my work with the Nonviolence and Children Program was to gather books we could use in our work, and to compile an annotated list so we could share these books with others.

I started slowly, reading and becoming familiar with children's books at the public library and at neighbor's homes. I also read books from booklists compiled by peace organizations. Most of these books did not impress me. Many were boring, preachy, and 'goody-goody,' containing a message which the author thought the children ought to learn. I talked with friends, parents and librarians, and soon they began coming to me with new suggestions for books and for other people to talk to.

There were some books which I really enjoyed, but I couldn't tell if children would enjoy them, too. So I read these books to my neighbors, Rachel and Beth Morris, ages five and eight, for their reactions They were glad to help.

"We liked helping you with your work and sharing books with you," they commented. "It was nice to have you read us stories and be able to walk into your house and read them to ourselves. When we found out what kind of books you wanted, we started bringing over books on our own to share with you."

Information is still coming in, and it was hard to stop here.* Please use the resources section to pick up where I left off.

—*Ellen Forsythe*

*Because so much of the information for this list came by word of mouth, there are many people to thank for their help. Included are Eleanor Perry, Eileen Abrams, Beth Morris and Rachel Morris.

Annotated Bibliography*

Conflict Resolution

Blaine, Marge, *The Terrible Thing That Happened at Our House*, Parents Magazine Press, N.Y., 1975, hb $5.50. Grades 2-4. (Also good on sex roles.)

Mom goes back to work, and then everything starts to change. One of the children runs away and the family has a meeting to work out solutions to everyone's difficulties.

Chapman, Kim Westsmith, *The Magic Hat,* Lollipop Power, Inc., Chapel Hill, N.C., 1973, pb $2.00. Grades 2-5. (Also good on sex roles.)

A "busybody" builds a fence separating the boys and the "masculine" toys from the girls and "their" toys. The children are unhappy with this division and decide to get rid of the fence.

Charders, Janet and Michael Foreman, *The General*, Routledge & Kegan, Boston, 1961, hb $6.85. Grades K-3.

An aggressive general who wants to become famous, does so after discovering the beauty of nature. He sends his soldiers home to return to their old jobs, thus creating a beautiful country which others come to admire.

Clymer, Eleanor, *The Big Pile of Dirt*, Holt, Rinehart & Winston, N.Y., 1968, hb $4.79, pb $.95. Grades preschool-3.

A pile of dirt is the only good place that the poor children have to play. Some rich people who are trying to beautify the city want it removed. The children find a way to keep their pile of dirt.

Hamanda, Hirusuke, *The Tears of the Dragon*, Parents Magazine Press, N.Y., 1967, hb $4.95. Grades K-3. (Also good on feelings.)

One boy does not believe the village rumor that the dragon who lives on the mountain is evil. He decides to invite the dragon to his birthday party. This book points out the role of misinformation and prejudice in creating walls.

Hutchins, Pat, *Changes, Changes,* Collier Books, N.Y., 1971, pb $.95. Grades preschool and up.

This outstanding picture book has no words. A wooden toy couple build their own house. When it burns down, they work together creatively to rebuild it elsewhere.

Lionni, Leo, *Swimmy,* Random House, Inc., N.Y., 1963, hb $4.95, pb $1.25. Grades preschool-2.

The small red fish are afraid to go anywhere because the big fish will eat them. Swimmy organizes them to swim together looking like one big fish.

---

* Prices and publishing information here are as of July, 1976. We suggest checking *Books in Print* before ordering.

Lobel, Anita, *Potatoes, Potatoes,* Harper and Row, N.Y., 1967, beautiful illustrations, hb $4.79. Grades K-3.

This is a story of war and a woman who refuses to take part in it. Her two sons join opposite armies; they come home with their hungry armies to eat potatoes. This book clearly points out the futility of war and the hardships it creates.

Pinkwater, Manus, *Bear's Picture*, Holt, Rinehart & Winston, N.Y., 1972, pb $1.45 (A Holt Owlet Book). Grades preschool-2.

A bear paints a colorful picture. Teased and disapproved of by two "fine, proper gentlemen," he remains happy with the picture he paints, and true to himself.

Sarah, Becky, *Fanshen, the Magic Bear*, New Seed Press, Stanford, Calif., 1973, pb $1.25. Grades 4-7. (Also good on sex roles.)

After talking to the Magic Bear, Laura convinces the people to stop cooperating with the oppressive king.

Dr. Seuss, *The Lorax*, Random House, N.Y., 1971, hb $3.95. Grades K and up.

The "once-ler" describes the results of his local business; the destruction of the local environment. This story does not answer the problem of pollution, but suggests that the one remaining truffula tree seed, in combination with care, is the only hope.

Wondriska, William, *John John Twilliger*, Holt, Rinehart & Winston, N.Y., 1966, pb $1.25. Grades 2-4. (Also good on feelings.)

John John cannot live by the rules that the Machine Gun Man has set up for the town, and he ends up changing the Machine Gun Man and the town. It becomes clear that people do not need to put up with irrational and repressive rules.

Feelings

Blue, Rose, *Grandma Didn't Wave Back,* Franklin Watts, Inc., N.Y., 1972, hb $4.95, Dell & Co., N.Y., pb $.95. Grades 3-5.

Debbie learns to deal with her Grandma's increasing senility on a day-to-day basis.

Blue, Rose, *A Month of Sundays,* Franklin Watts, Inc., N.Y., 1974, hb $4.95. Grades 3-5.

This is the story of a boy whose family separates. He must make new relationships with both his parents, and find a whole new lifestyle.

Crawford, Sue Hefferman, *Minoo's Family*, Canadian Women's Educational Press, Waterloo, Ontario, 1974, pb $2.75. Grades 1-4.

Minoo, whose parents are separating, deals with her feelings of loneliness, anger and confusion.

Estes, Eleanore, *A Little Oven,* Harcourt, Brace & World, Inc., N.Y., 1955, hb $4.50. Grades preschool-3. (Traditional sex roles.)

This story describes a mother learning from her child the need for physical affection.

Hazen, Nancy, *Grownups Cry, Too*, Lollipop Power, Inc., Chapel Hill, N.C., 1973, pb $1.75. Grades K-3.

Description of different situations in which people cry.

Jewett, Sarah Orne, *A White Heron,* Thomas Crowell Co., N.Y., 1963, hb $4.25. Grades 4-6.

A girl must decide whether or not to show her friend, the hunter, the nest of her favorite bird. This story points out moral choices that people must make.

Keats, Ezra Jack, *Letter to Amy,* Harper & Row, N.Y., 1968, hb $5.95. Grades K-3.

A boy decides to chance the ridicule of his friends and invite a girl to his birthday party.

Keats, Ezra Jack, *Peter's Chair,* Harper & Row, N.Y., 1967, hb $5.95. Grades K-2. (Traditional sex roles.)

Peter is angry because his parents are painting *his* crib to give to his baby sister.

Mann, Peggy, *My Dad Lives in a Downtown Hotel*, Avalon Books, N.Y., 1973, hb $4.50, pb $.95. Grades 5-6.

Joey blames himself for his parents' separation. He learns to accept that it is not his fault, and that the separation is good for his parents.

McGovern, Ann, *Little Wolf,* Scholastic Book Services, N.Y., 1965, hb $3.75. Grades K-3.

An Indian boy is ridiculed for not wanting to be a hunter and a warrior, until he saves the life of the chief's only son.

Miles, Misha, *Annie and the Old One*, Little, Brown & Co., Boston, 1971, hb $5.95. Grades 2-4.

The story of Annie, a young Navajo, learning to accept the impending death of her beloved grandmother.

Parish, Barb, *Families Grow in Different Ways*, Canadian Women's Education Press, Toronto, Ontario, pb $1.75. Grades K-2.

Sara and Jamie are waiting for their new siblings to arrive. Jamie's mother is pregnant, and Sara's family is adopting.

Stanek, Muriel, *I Won't Go Without a Father*, Albert Whitman & Co., Chicago, 1972, hb $3.95. Grades 1-4.

Steve won't go to the school open house because he is embarrassed that he does not have a father.

Stein, Sara Bonnett, *A Hospital Story*, photography by Dick Frank, Open Family Series, Walker & Co., N.Y., 1972, hb $5.95.

This book is written for children and adults to read together, about a girl's tonsilectomy. It encourages adults and children to discuss their fears about hospitals.

Stein, Sara Bonnett, *About Dying*, photography by Dick Frank, Open Family Series, Walker & Co., N.Y., 1974, hb $5.95.

Written for children and adults to read together, this book talks about death in a very open way and encourages questions.

(Other Open Family Series books at the same price include *About Handicaps, Making Babies, That New Baby.*)

Steptoe, John, *Stevie*, Harper & Row, N.Y., 1969, hb $4.95. Grades preschool-3.

Although Stevie was a pest, when he moves away Robert misses him, and appreciates the good times they had together.

Surowiecki, Sandra Lucas, *Joshua's Day,* Lollipop Power, Inc., Chapel Hill, N.C., 1972, pb $1.75. Grades preschool-1.

Joshua gets angry when his block tower is knocked over. After screaming and crying, he is able to continue building. Later his mother listens as he talks about it more. This book recognizes that people have angry feelings and describes how Joshua deals with his own.

Tester, Sylvia, *Moods and Emotions*, David C. Cook Publishing Co., Elgin, Ill., 1970, $5.50. Grades K-3. (13 in. x 18 in. packet)

Teaching pictures recommended for Headstart—16 photographs and 40-page resource booklet. Open-ended stories to go with the pictures, which let children finish the stories; also complete stories which can stand on their own or be discussed.

Turkle, Brinton, *The Fiddler of High Lonesome*, Viking Press, N.Y., 1968, hb $6.50. Grades 2-4.

Bochamp, the fiddler, won't participate in killing animals. This is shocking to his relatives with whom he has gone to live.

Viorst, Judith, *The Tenth Good Thing About Barney*, Atheneum, N.Y., 1974, hb $4.95, pb $1.25. Grades K-4.

Children have a funeral for a cat and remember the things they liked about him.

Feelings (continued)

Waber, Bernard, *Ira Sleeps Over*, Houghton, Mifflin Co., Boston, 1972, hb $4.95, pb $1.25. Grades K-3. (Also good on sex roles.)

Ira struggles to decide whether or not to take his teddy bear when he goes to spend the night at a friend's house.

Watson, Jane Warner, Robert E. Switzer, M.D., and J. Cotter Hirschbarg, M.D., *Sometimes I Get Angry,* Golden Press, N.Y., 1971, hb $1.95. Age 2-3½. (This book reads most easily with discussion at end of each page.)

This book acquaints adults and chidren with the problems that develop as a part of early growth. It can stimulate discussions between adults and children.

Zolotow, Charlotte, *The Hating Book*, Harper & Row, N.Y., 1969, hb $5.95. Grades preschool-3.

A close friendship almost falls apart because of a misunderstanding. This book points out the responsibility of each person in a relationship to say how she or he is feeling.

Zolotow, Charlotte, *The Quarreling Book*, Harper & Row, N.Y., 1963, hb $4.95. Grades K-3. (Traditional sex roles.)

One person's bad mood makes the next person angry. Soon the entire family is making nasty comments at each other until someone breaks the spiral.

Sex Roles

dePoix, Carol, *Jo, Flo and Yolanda,* Lollipop Power, Inc., Chapel Hill, N.C., 1973, pb $1.75. Ages 3-7.

Jo, Flo and Yolanda are triplets with a lot in common, but they are also very different.

Fitzhugh, Louise, *Harriet the Spy,* Dell Publishing Co., N.Y., 1964, pb $1.25. Grades 5 and up.

An hilarious, often touching story of an independent, curious, and totally honest girl who has the misfortune of having her secret notebook found by her classmates.

Hart, Carole, *Delilah*, Harper & Row, N.Y., 1973, hb $4.43. Grades 2-6. (Also good on feelings.)

This is the story of a girl whose life is free from traditional sex role expectations. One chapter is included in the "Free To Be You and Me" songbook and record.

Klein, Norma, *Mom, the Wolf Man and Me,* Avon Books, N.Y., 1972, hb $5.95, pb $.95. Grades 4-6. (Also good on feelings.)

Brett enjoys not having a father, but worries that her mother may marry and become "normal." This book describes Brett's fear of losing her special relationship with her mother.

Levy, Elizabeth, *Nice Little Girls*, Delacorte Press, N.Y., 1974, hb $5.95. Grades K-3.

Jackie challenges her teacher's assumptions by insisting that it is okay for her to build boxes even though she is a girl.

Levinson, Irene, *Peter Learns to Crochet*, The New Seed Press, Stanford, Calif., 1973, pb $1.25. Grades 3-5. (Also good on feelings.) Also included in the Feminist Press *Storypack,* Old Westbury, N.Y., 1974, pb $2.50. Grades pre-school-5.

Peter searches everywhere to find someone to teach him to crochet; just as he is about to give up, his male teacher offers to show him how.

Merriam, Eve, *Mommies at Work*, Scholastic Book Services, N.Y., 1961, pb $.95. Grades K-2.

This is a picture book, depicting mothers doing everything from washing dishes to building bridges. Reading this book brings out stereotypes that children have. They often respond: "Mommies can't do that!"

O'Dell, Scott, *Island of the Blue Dolphins*, Dell Publishing Co., N.Y., 1960, hb $7.95, pb $1.25. Grades 5-9.

After her people leave, an Indian girl who remains on the island learns to hunt and fish as well as doing "women's" work.

Rich, Gibson, *Firegirl*, The Feminist Press, N.Y., 1972, pb $3.00. Grades 2-4. (Also good on feelings.)

Despite the disapproval of her parents, Brenda wants to be a fireman. She proves she can do the job when she saves a rabbit from a burning house.

Rivera, Edith Vonnegut, *Nora's Tale*, Richard W. Baron, N.Y., 1973, hb $3.95. Grades 1-6. (Also good on feelings and conflict resolution.)

Nora creates a beautiful world that Bertha tries to destroy. Nora thinks of a way to solve this problem.

Stimm, Claus, *Three Strong Women: A Tale from Japan*, The Viking Press, N.Y., 1962, pb $.95. Grades 2-5.

This is a tall-tale about a proud Japanese wrestler; he meets three strong women who change his life.

Zolotow, Charlotte, *William's Doll*, Harper & Row, N.Y., 1972, hb $4.95. Grades K-3. (Also included in the *Free To Be You and Me* record and songbook.)

William's desire for a doll distresses his parents and his friends. His grandmother encourages William and gives him a doll.

Other Materials That Are Good in Sex Roles

The Feminist Press, *Storypack,* Old Westbury, N.Y., 1974, pb $2.50. Grades pre-school-5.

The *Storypack* includes five stories for different age levels: "My Body Feels Good," "Living with Mommy," "Peter Learns to Crochet," "When It Flooded the Elementary School," and "The Strange Hocket Family." This packet also includes a teacher/parent manual with suggested questions and activities related to the stories.

Thomas, Marlo, et al., *Free To Be You and Me,* McGraw-Hill Book Co., N.Y., 1974, pb $5.95, record $5.89.

"A celebration of laughter, love, and freedom of choice for all children, whatever their age, race or sex."

Resources

Below are listed small presses which publish good children's books. They will send bibliographies on request, for a minimal fee.

- **Before We Are Six,** 12 Bridgeport Road East, Waterloo, Ontario, Canada.

  Before We Are Six publishes inexpensive paperbacks about family life: one-parent families, separation, and non-nuclear family situations. Their books are good for expressing feelings.

  Before We Are Six is a part of the Canadian Women's Educational Press, 280 Bloor Street West, Suite 305, Toronto, Ontario, Canada

- **The Feminist Press,** Box 334, Old Westbury, New York 11568.

  This alternative publishing house is "working in many different ways to create more meaningful learning experiences for girls and boys, for women and men ...[and] renewed respect for women, their learning, and their literature."

- **Lollipop Power, Inc.,** P.O. Box 1171, Chapel Hill, N.C. 27514.

  "Lollipop Power is a feminist collective working to overcome sex role stereotypes in the lives of children. In addition to publishing books, we are reaching educators, parents, and children through workshops and multi-media presentations."

- **New Seed Press,** P.O. Box 3016, Stanford, Calif. 94305.

  These are friendly and informative people, publishing non-sexist children's books that are also good in their portrayal of conflict resolution and feelings.

Outstanding Authors

While compiling this booklist, we found that some authors write one or two good books, while others write one excellent book after another. The authors listed below, we found, write excellently and consistently. We would recommend almost any book these authors write.

Rose Blue	Leo Lioni	Judith Viorst
Norma Klein	Scott O'Dell	William Wondriska
Anita Lobel	Brinton Turkle	Charlotte Zolotow
Arnold Lobel		

In sixth grade, we read Greek myths. I read the stories over and over trying to find some formula for pleasing all the gods. But if I chose Athene as my patron, Hera would be jealous; if a sacrifice were made to Apollo, Dionysus was apt to cause trouble. Slowly the truth of the myths seeped in—I could not please everyone all the time. Life as the new kid in school started to be easier.

I have always loved fairy tales. Certainly there were scary parts, but read over and over with a parent at bedtime, an anxiety faced was an anxiety conquered. Dragons (of fear) could be slain! Simpletons (with whom I identified) could inherit the kingdom! *I* wasn't scared when adults grinned down at me with big teeth and said I looked good enough to eat. If they tried anything, Hansel and Gretel had shown me what to do. So while I cheer the growing list of books for children that address their real-life feelings and dilemmas, I hope we will not ignore the legacy of fairy tales, legends and myths, for they deal with the deepest issues of maturation, too, but in symbolic form.

As a writer for children, I read the work of scholars who differ enormously in their interpretation of fairy tales. The variety of their interpretation indicates to me the stories' greatest strength; fairy tales are as receptive to the projections of a three-year-old or an adolescent as they are to scholars of a Freudian, Jungian, or behaviorist bent. Take Rapunzel, for instance. One friend, a four-year-old boy who lives in a household of feisty siblings and warring parents, responds to the safety of the tower and the fact that Rapunzel could use her own body—her hair—to change her situation. For a girl approaching adolescence, the story can reassure her that a jealous mother will not be able to thwart a girl's need to explore. Yet the poet Anne Sexton begins her narrative poem "Rapunzel" with the words, "A woman / who loves a woman / is forever young."!

And so fairy tales—and sometimes other imaginative storytelling too—reflect the archetypal dilemmas of each of our growing, be they Oedipal conflicts or the integration of an unconscious aspect of the Self. As Bruno Bettleheim has said, fairy tales reveal "truth as valid today as it was once upon a time."

—*Mally Cox-Chapman*

Old Favorites

Editor's Note: *Below are books written in the past thirty years or so which have already become "old favorites" among children and adults. The annotations indicate into which one or more of our three categories each book falls.*

Burnett, Francess Hodgson, *The Secret Garden,* Dell Publishing Co., N.Y., 1971, pb $1.50. Grades 4 and up. (feelings)

A girl discovers that life is exciting, that she likes herself and living. She finds a way to share these new discoveries with her invalid cousin.

DeAngeli, Marguerite, *Thee Hannah*, Doubleday, N.Y., 1940, hb $5.95. Grades 4-6. (feelings)

After helping some escaped slaves, a girl becomes proud of her family's beliefs.

DeSaint Exupery, Antoine, *The Little Prince,* Harcourt, Brace, Jovanovich, N.Y., 1943, hb $5.95, pb $1.50. Grades 3-7. (feelings)

A touching story of a boy who teaches a lonely man about caring.

Konigsburg, E.L., *From the Mixed-up Files of Mrs. Basil E. Frankweiler,* Atheneum, N.Y., 1967, pb $1.50. Grades 4-6. (sex roles)

A girl leaves home with her younger brother to live in the New York Metropolitan Museum of Art.

Lindgren, Astrid, *Pippi Longstocking*, The Viking Press, N.Y., 1950, hb $3.95, pb $.95. Grades 4-6. (sex roles)

Pippi is an adventuresome, strong and exciting girl. She lives in a house alone and along with her two neighbors she does many crazy things.

Leaf, Munro, *The Story of Ferdinand*, Viking Press, N.Y., 1936, hb $2.95, pb $.95. Grades K-3. (sex roles and conflict resolution)

The story of a peaceful, strong bull who would rather smell flowers than fight.

L'Engle, Madeline, *A Wrinkle in Time*, Dell Publishing Co., N.Y., 1962, pb $1.25. Grades 4-8. (sex roles)

Meg travels through outer space to find her father. Meg also has a delightful friendship with her mother who is a scientist.

McGovern, Ann, *The Runaway Slave: The Story of Harriet Tubman*, Scholastic Book Services, N.Y., 1965, pb $.95. Grades 2-3. (sex roles and conflict resolution)

This is the story of Harriet's liberation from slavery and her struggles to help others.

Piper, Watty, *The Little Engine That Could*, Platt & Munk, Inc., 1961, hb $3.95, pb $1.95. Grades preschool-3. (conflict resolution and feelings)

A train was stuck. All the large engines that went by refused to help it over the mountain. A small engine that had never been over the mountain itself came to the rescue while saying to itself, "I think I can."

Williams, Margery, *The Velveteen Rabbit*, Doubleday & Co., Garden City, N.Y., 1958, hb $3.95, pb $1.75. Grades 2-5. (feelings)

A story of a beloved stuffed animal who becomes real through love.

White, E.B., *Charlotte's Web,* illus. Garth Williams, Harper & Row, N.Y., 1952, hb $4.95, pb $1.25. Grades 2-4. (sex roles and feelings)

The story of Charlotte, a compassionate spider who saves the life of a pet pig.

Wondriska, William, *The Tomato Patch*, Holt, Rinehart & Winston, N.Y., 1964, hb $3.50. Grades 2-4. (conflict resolution)

A young girl's tomato convinces two warring kingdoms to stop fighting and start farming.

Conclusion

"Groups of confident, caring, problem-solving people who are reaching out to others around them" is a vision which a friend of the Nonviolence and Children Program shared with us recently. We hope that this manual nurtures such people.

A mindset of affirmation, an ability to share feelings, information, and experiences, a confidence to work at resolving conflict, and a sense of community... these all contradict feelings of helplessness or powerlessness. As we contradict these feelings, we are able to act constructively for change. The first part of the manual, (pp. 1-48) lays the groundwork for empowering children and adults to act.

The latter part of the manual is a beginning for action. Imagine the consequences, for instance, if a school faculty used the consensus decision-making method outlined in Berit Lakey's section on "Meeting Facilitation" (p. 79). A stronger sense of community might follow, and a real belief that each individual can contribute to making change. What might happen if a family followed Lois Dorn's example ("Magic Meetings," p. 77) to adapt what seemed appropriate for it from the manual's approaches?

We began the manual by stating that adults have "tremendous power in children's lives and over children's facilities to handle conflict." We've emphasized ways in which *adults* can help *children* to develop nonviolent attitudes and skills. Let's imagine the effect on *everybody* when adults develop and use these attitudes and skills with each other. A family changes remarkably when parents, grandparents, aunts, uncles and friends consistently respect and affirm themselves and each other, as well as the children. A school is transformed when the faculty, administration, and supporting services make a point to appreciate each other and to share feelings, experiences, and skills. We all deserve to treat ourselves this way, and positive changes will occur when we do.

Not just families and schools, but daycare centers, agencies, hospitals, and other institutions may offer you the opportunity to develop skills, create models, and reach out to make new friends and allies in order to transform situations. Wherever you are, you can:

- interrupt destructive ways of relating to people, and
- create new models as positive alternatives.

What Next?

If you are interested in this manual, chances are that you have already reached a certain level of awareness about children and adults and change. You have been looking around for friends and allies to share your concerns; maybe you've already found them. You may be seeking a total transformation of society, or you may be concerned with improving a particular situation. Whatever your goal, do take time to appreciate yourself and your work and to ask "What next?"

The writers of this manual have been asking ourselves this question, too. In study groups, and in our individual work, we've been asking such questions as:

- How can parents and teachers regard each other as allies and advocates for children, instead of seeing each other as adversaries?

- What if all the like-minded people in our area joined together to work with each other, share resources, and apply political pressure to achieve our goals? How can we help this to come about?

- What are the connections between the way young people are treated in our society and the way it is organized economically?

- How are people in other parts of the world working on the same problems? What do we have to learn from each other?

- What do we want the world to be like for ourselves and for children? What can we do today, tomorrow, and next year, in five, ten, and twenty years in order to make it happen?

114

Appendix

For the Fun of It!

Selected Cooperative Games for Children and Adults

By Marta Harrison
and
The Nonviolence and Children Program

ABOUT THE AUTHOR

As a member of the Friends Peace Committee Collective for the past two years, Marta Harrison has co-led games workshops and numerous Nonviolence and Children Training Seminars for teachers. For the Fun of It *grew out of that experience.*

But the REAL reason Marta is the author of this book is that she is a lover of songs (particularly rounds), and games (all of them!) and laughter. So while everyone in the Collective—and many others—contributed to For the Fun of It, *this book reflects Marta: her commitment to non-hierarchical ways for adults and children to work together; her intense interest in the true nature of the learning process; her joy in living simply and in community.*

Reflecting Marta is a great compliment to this book.

> *Mally Cox-Chapman, a member of*
> *the Nonviolence and Children Subcommittee*

Beyond Competition: A Search for Excellence

For two years, since I became involved with cooperative games, I have questioned and wondered about the role competition plays in our culture. No longer enjoying most competitive games, I feel uncomfortable and dissatisfied when I am a "winner." It's important to me, now, that everyone feel included, that everyone is participating equally, and most of all, that everyone is having a good time.

However, it is also very important that I strive for excellence, that which is inwardly deeply satisfying. But how can I excel if I do not compete? My own traditional "schooling," leaving much to be desired, was based on competition. My more recent learning experiences lead me to share some of my evolving ideas about achieving excellence without competition.

American education today, in its approach to all things great and small, lacks reverence—respect for life. And the future of education must lie in an attempt to convey knowledge and skills in a new way, an artistic and religious way, so that every detail awakens reverence, awakens respect... reverence is to the soul what food is to the body. It is the ground of all true feelings; it is the beginning of wisdom; it is also the beginning of power.... It is through reverence that we learn to know the depth and fullness of life, so that the multiplication of trivial knowledge is quieted down and given direction. [1]

These words touch me deeply. They represent an attitude, a quality of experience to reach for, to remember while struggling to learn new skills. Reverence and respect for life are basic to the ways I approach learning and striving for excellence. From my own intense interaction with clay (later described more fully), I have, indeed, come to know a little more about the "depth and fullness" of life. This quote reflects what I, within myself, still only dimly feel to be true. It provides an outline of a standard of excellence to work towards.

Reverence for life involves appreciating our own innate gifts. If we respect life, we respect the life within ourselves, within others. It is important to be all I can be and to attempt to bring out the best in others; then they, in turn, can help others to do their best to strive for excellence.

How can we reach for excellence without putting others down? Americans are used to thinking of competition as the best way to strive for excellence. But is it?

Excellence is attained through seeking and recognizing one's own abilities and giving them enough attention to develop to their fullest. It is achieved through wanting to learn a new skill or craft or sport so badly that an inner commitment is made, calling forth determination to see it through. Excellence is achieved through caring, doing something for its own sake. George Leonard says, "What we run for we shall never reach, and that is the heart and glory of it. In the end, running is its own reward. It can never be justified. We run for the sake of running, nothing more." [2]

The struggle between the learning and the individual is an intense, sometimes rewarding, sometimes frustrating process. I persist only because it matters to me, not because it is important to my teacher, not because there is a gold medal, not because I have to be a winner. I am more interested in the quality of what I am doing than in winning or being the best. It may be a craft, a period of history, a sport, a cause such as environmental concerns. It may end up being something that others recognize as excellent and that they admire me for. Or it may be something that only I recognize as valuable.

We can find historical precedents within our own country. The Native Americans' tradition is reverence for life and striving for excellence in all that they do. They believe in the education of the whole person which begins at home. Children, taught to have reverence for all life, learn how this creates the need for excellence.

117

It is the excellence of every detail in an art or craft, and the thoughts behind it that count. Children must be taught in such a way that they set to work with that same real seriousness with which Mrs. Old Coyote does her bead work, even if they do not achieve such beautiful results. [3]

Their approach is based on a belief that all of life teaches, that everyone, whether child or adult, is constantly learning. It is a natural part of living, not confined to "school" or childhood. They, indeed, have a rich source of knowledge and respect for life that other Americans could learn a great deal from.

White settlers in this country ruthlessly ignored Native American values. Instead, competition as a means to achieve excellence has rooted itself in the modern world and, consequently, has affected the quality of human interaction and the quality of education of the whole person. It has become a destructive means of striving for excellence. How has this happened?

Competition implies a winner; it also implies a loser. Competition means the best, the most. It must also mean the worst, the least. Competition means A's, honors, degrees; it must also mean F's, failures and dropouts. Competition means an imposed set of standards by which one is judged a success or a failure. We have all been "taught" to value the end result of the game, or the A, or the big promotion more than the joy of the effort we make.

Competition keeps us separate from each other. If I need recognition for my work, I have to be the best. I can't afford to share my expertise with anyone. The barriers thus erected keep me isolated and alone in my glory.

The desire to win keeps us from seeing what competition does to the losers—to the poor, to the outcasts, to the sick and to the aged of our rich, successful society. The existence of these "leftover people" means that some humans have more power over their lives than others. Competition tends to ignore the humanness of people and the unique individuality within each one of us. It has become a way of life for everyone, including the "losers" who are still trying to win, and even those who have hopelessly given up.

And yet, competition has provided objective standards which are helpful and important. Jim Ryun, the well-known long-distance runner, used the previous world record for running the mile as a standard against which he measured his own progress. After consciously de-

ciding to break the record, he worked hard to do it and was successful. But "he did not run those thousands of miles in order to glorify himself. It is enough of a reward to be satisfied within." [4]

His fellow runners said that Jim had to have the "killer instinct" in order to win. Jim stated that he wanted to treat his competitors as friends and have respect between him and them. He was not interested in psyching anyone out. Although he ran alongside other people, Jim's attitude was not a personal one of "beating the other guy," but one of doing his best to "beat" the objective time clock. Jim proved that it was his deep, burning desire for greatness, not a "killer instinct," that motivated him to surpass his own limits and the limits of others.

Such an attitude would allow competition to be a healthy, dynamic element in sports, providing humane supportiveness, instead of cut-throat vindictiveness. Jim Ryun provides a model of a person who, with the help of objective standards, succeeded in being "satisifed within" and achieved excellence by being challenged and reaching for the outer limits of his abilities.

For myself, I had been deeply disappointed in my school and college years without ever understanding why. I knew only outer-directed goals and had no idea of the intrinsic rewards of an activity or skill. I was the kind of person who was initially interested in learning many things, but, once past the easy euphoric beginning, I became exceedingly frustrated and simply gave up due to a lack of know-how, support and inner resources. Needless to say, my own schooling had neglected to "teach" me the meaningful joys of learning.

Fortunately, about five years ago, someone very dear to me suggested I join a beginning clay class. I had had no previous experience with clay and was literally terrified. But the teacher, Shirley Tassencourt, emphasized neither technique nor product. I was encouraged to watch and observe what happened to the clay as my hands gingerly pushed and pulled at it, and then to react from deep within myself while letting my fumbling fingers shape and mold the clay. My first tentative attempts exposed so much doubt and so much negativism that I was like the six-year-olds I've observed, hating and wanting to wreck my own work. I felt vulnerable and inexperienced, sometimes extremely child-like in my reactions.

Shirley was extraordinarily sensitive and

118

supportive, a "natural-born" teacher. She gradually brought out the essence in each person; she gently nourished into being forgotten aspects of myself. She valued what I, Marta, had to offer and what I was as a person. It seemed as if the wet ugly clay represented an ugly part of me, as I awkwardly tried to shape it into a bowl. It also seemed to represent a beautiful part of me that Shirley was able constantly to reflect back to me until I could finally appreciate what she meant.

That year for the first time I inwardly experienced the learning process. Something was transformed within me and manifested itself in the clay pieces. I am now (five years later) beginning to accept my own work, to value and appreciate it. Some empty space within me has been filled, and I realize that all my life I had craved this kind of deep learning experience. Because of my longing to learn about clay and pots, even when I wanted to give up, I couldn't. I was creating my own inner desire for excellence.

Each person requires different conditions in learning something new. I personally need a great deal of time and space, both mental and physical, and a teacher who gives me room to experiment, who is available for questions and technical assistance, and who is sensitive enough to know when to speak to my frustrations. In experiencing such a creative learning process in the clay class, I came to value myself more highly. I feel enriched and more settled as an individual. I want this kind of experience for every child and adult.

Perhaps we adults who are in the position of "teaching" or relating to children of any age should be thoroughly immersed, ourselves, in the process of learning something new for its own sake. Then we could more easily understand how to begin to establish in young people a hunger for intense, joyful, life-long learning experiences. It is important that we reach for those special qualities and gifts which make children unique and creative. It means encouraging them to find an interesting activity or skill that excites them and then providing support when the frustrations occur. Then, gradually, young people may come to depend more on an internal sense of what is right and less on an external standard of success.

"But how can children be motivated to involve themselves in something if there isn't some sort of reward at the end?" asks the anxious parent or teacher. We adults fear that children do not care about learning. We think we must push and shove them around because we "know what is best for them." But children are far more capable than we think they are. Piaget and others have demonstrated that, from babyhood on, children are constantly learning what they need to know. A great deal of learning occurs through play, which is children's work. They **want** to learn how to read, write and understand numbers—in their own time and when the need or desire arises.

I know of an unusual example of a child taking charge of his own environment and learning experiences. He was in the first grade of public school, falling asleep at his desk and generally unresponsive to the teacher. His parents sent him to visit a private school, where I taught, for a week in early May in preparation for enrollment in the fall. When he realized he would have to return to public school to finish the year, he clearly stated in no uncertain terms that he would not go back, that he would stay at the new school. His parents and the school agreed.

Because he was in a flexible learning environment, he was allowed to postpone learning how to read, although this created a great deal of anxiety for his parents. He explored the outdoors, shared his extensive knowledge of weeds and plants with anyone who would listen, brought in all sorts of interesting rocks, and gathered assorted junk which he eventually made into fascinating machines. His personality and attitude endeared him to all of us. This intelligent boy was simply following his own need. Six months later, he asked for a book and began to learn how to read. He was searching for his own excellence, doing what was internally satisfying in an environment conducive to honoring the uniqueness of each person.

The desire to learn is natural with all human beings. Yet learning does not happen easily in structured, curriculum-run schools. Often an outside, imposed curriculum frustrates the unique learning process of the individual. Because learning is an innate part of living, frustrations in learning can upset the inner sense of self-direction. Too often, the American school system as it functions today increases the level of frustration to the point of no return, helping to create the lack of interest which develops at about the second or third grade. Gradually, as children progress through the elementary years, the outer, superficial rewards replace the rewards of inner satisfaction

[Traditionally,] the schools stand as a buttress against uniqueness, a

119

monument to the great American melting pot. In spite of official deference to the ideals of pluralism and the sanctity of the individual, we submit our children to a process of socialization that is almost always mistrustful of the child's own personal goals.[5]

The sad and inhumane consequence of all this "institutionalized mistrust of children" is that the child's self-worth is judged by outer standards of grades, tests, memorization skills, compliance to arbitrary and unfair rules, etc. Fears, feelings of inadequacies, low self-esteem, hopelessness are all blocks that sensitive teachers and parents constantly fight against, but they are born out of the great lack of opportunity for the child to pursue his or her own goals.

*We, as adults, have a responsibility to help children regard themselves as worthwhile and valuable people. The teacher or parent, assuming that children are eager to learn, must nour-*ish each little spark of interest, no matter what it is. We don't have to urge children to compete for excellence; it is created from within. Children who are allowed to seek and nurture their own inner-directed interests will be more likely to grow up into self-reliant, clear-thinking, whole individuals.*

*Commitment to excellence as a way of life would mean each one of us, adults and children, being all we could be, developing our abilities to the fullest. It would mean being involved in any activity, whether mountain climbing or weeding the garden, for its own sake. It would mean that winning would cease to be a **reason** for participating in work or play. It would mean supporting and appreciating one another as we grapple with the challenges of life and the tasks we take on. With a deep commitment to excellence, a respect and reverence for life would gradually emerge and become a basis for daily living and a foundation for meaningful, rewarding learning experiences.*

Marta Harrison

Philadelphia, Pa.
July, 1976

REFERENCES

1. Sylvester M. Morey and Oliva L. Gilliam, *Respect for Life*, New York: Waldorf Press, 1974, p. 197.
2. George Leonard, *The Ultimate Athlete*, New York: The Viking Press, 1975, p. 189.
3. Morey and Gilliam, *Respect for Life*, p. 192.
4. Cordner Nelson, *The Jim Ryun Story*, Los Altos: Tafnews Press, 1967, p. 258.
5. Myron Arms and David Denman, *Touching the World*, New York: Charles Scribner's Sons, 1975, p. 99.

About five years ago...

...a group of Friends (Quakers) interested in bringing education in nonviolence to young children started the Friends Peace Committee's Nonviolence and Children Program. We are now a small working group of five—Stephanie Judson, Chuck Esser, Karen Zaur, Ellen Deacon and Lois Dorn (replacing Marta Harrison)—and a dynamic subcommittee of parents and educators, all concerned with finding ways to create a nonviolent, supportive environment which allows children to be nourished into caring, loving, active adults.

We believe that children up to junior high school age are more interested in the politics of their families and classrooms than in the politics of Cambodia or legislative hearings. ("You give back that book, or I'm telling!" "Teacher, she just broke my pencil!") Since the individual, the family, and the classroom are, in many ways, microcosms of the larger society, we are searching for creative, nonviolent activities and solutions in these areas. By working against the verbal violence, the "put-downs," and the unloving, hurtful interactions of people at these fundamental levels, we believe we can affect the larger society in an important way.

The Nonviolence and Children Program has several goals:
1) to develop an atmosphere of affirmation;
2) to create an atmosphere where feelings can be shared and respected;
3) to build a sense of community, of mutual support and caring;
4) to teach problem-solving skills;
5) to share our sense of joy in life and in others.

June, 1976, marks the end of a three-year school program funded by the Peace Committee of the Philadelphia Yearly Meeting. We began in Friends' (Quaker) schools but also found ways to reach out to two neighborhood public schools. We have given workshops for school faculties, day care centers, mental health clinics, a Headstart program, college students, parents and Friends.

The program has grown tremendously. It started with three people in one classroom; now it is an ever-widening circle of people who care deeply about children and the quality of human relationships. We have been very careful not to act as established experts. We prefer to think of ourselves (the working group) as facilitators, providing space for people to share ideas, attitudes, skills, tools and techniques. The program is based on an equal exchange of ideas between us and those individuals we have met throughout these three years. The result has been that people who would never have dreamed of co-leading a workshop have gotten up their courage and plunged ahead with excellent results.

The network is based on a peer relationship. We are all peers, because we are all learning from each other. Since there is no rigid, established way of doing things, the opportunity to contribute has created high morale and a gentle excitement that permeates the whole program. *For the Fun of It* is an excellent example of the enriching resources of teachers, parents and others who, with encouragement, spontaneously invent and create activities for their children. It has been deeply satisfying to be connected to this growing network, in which this handbook is a vital link.

A comprehensive description of the Nonviolence and Children Program's goals, philosophy and methods will soon be available in book form. Write to the Friends Peace Committee, 1515 Cherry St., Philadelphia, PA 19102.

Some thoughts about games and their uses

Games are really important. They are an opportunity to build a sense of community and trust within the classroom, in faculty meetings and with families. Children joyfully "play games" inside and out, with energy, laughter and seriousness. What may seem like frivolous and carefree behavior is really the children's way of learning about themselves, their environment and other people. As the children grow, they learn small and large muscular coordination, discover how to flex and move their bodies in ways set up by the rules of the game. They become adept at basic skills, such as running, jumping, stopping and starting quickly, standing still while someone looks for them. They learn to share toys and take turns, supporting each other, cooperating with a number of persons in order to play the game. Following rules and limits is a part of the learning process. If children are adapting and inventing their own games, they discover how to think and how to make limits cooperatively. They become involved in a group process, and they act on what they themselves have decided. They can then judge whether it works or not. Learning is a definite process, one that children become involved in naturally and intuitively.

Problems with games. Sometimes games are used thoughtlessly. An example is the stunt or trick used to break the ice; it is "fun" for everyone at the expense of one person. Many card games penalize those who don't think quickly or plan in advance. Elimination games are really only "fun" for the co-ordinated and fast players. The slow or awkward person who is always out on the first round is bound to accumulate "bad" experiences and may stop playing altogether. For instance, in Musical Chairs, people have to drop out when they don't get a chair. That means that the majority of people are not playing for most of the game, while the "better players" are competing for the prize.

Some thoughts on competition. In our culture, winning is a valued commodity. We all want to be successful in what we do and to be praised and appreciated for our efforts. Society doesn't provide many avenues for us to receive the recognition we need, so winning has become a primary means for getting

praise and attention. Smiling, congratulating attention is focused on the winner; losers are expected to be "good sports" or are kindly told, "Better luck next time." The winner feels good and/or apologetic, afraid that no one will like him or her or burdened with the group's or team's expectation that he or she will continue to win. The loser may feel many things—angry, determined to win next time at any cost, bitterly disappointed, not valued as a person. In this society, competition tends to create barriers between people; thus everyone loses. Insensitive use of games can be harmful to the group as a whole as well as to individuals.

Competition, in itself, can be beneficial in that it can help a child develop skills and measure himself or herself against the previous scores made. A group can work together to accomplish a task against an outside impersonal element such as the clock. The problem with competition, however, is the feelings that are connected to winning and losing. There are thoughtful and caring instructors of team sports who attempt to foster an attitude of good sportsmanship. But they have to work very hard to counteract the deeply ingrained reactions to winning and losing.

Nonviolence and Children Program use of games. Recognizing that these competitive elements exist, we use games to focus on establishing rapport and good group spirit with the children. Along with much affirming and becoming acquainted with individual children, we use cooperative activities to help build a feeling of support and caring in a group. Thinking about the participants and their needs, we have tried to weed out any games that leave people out, force children to compete against each other or participate unequally. With these "no win" games, we hope to create a kind of environment where everyone can work and play together without winning or losing being the criterion for success.

Adults can play, too. We need to play as much as children do. In many of the groups we are part of (at work, in church, committees and PTA), we don't have the natural energy-releasing connections to each other that children do and may, therefore, have more need of playful activities. It may be harder for us to participate in a simple active game, but once people have tried it, they really like it. As one teacher said, "I'll never forget the time when we were all down on the floor playing a silly game. We never had such a good time together before!"

There may be resistance to initiating a game because Western society has taught us to think of games as foolish, silly, and a waste of time. However, hundreds of grownups have played these activities among themselves in a variety of situations and have enjoyed them tremendously. They have brought people together through laughter, offered alternatives to competition, and established new, more human lines of communication. As a result, people are more relaxed and open with each other and better able to work as a unit. It's worth the extra effort.

Uses of the handbook. Recognizing that the teacher has a central role in the classroom, we hope that this handbook can be a help in thinking about new approaches to classroom dynamics. Because the teacher is intimately involved with the children in the room, he or she can best determine what is needed in any particular situation—to counteract a negative tone of boredom, hostility, etc. Every teacher has the capacity to deal creatively with such situations, to think up innovative ways of establishing a positive tone to help children learn together more effectively. The suggestions in this handbook are intended not to be a final authority but to provide a stimulus for thinking up new games and activities. Most of the activities below have been developed and successfully used by other teachers. Many are adaptations of old standbys. We hope that this handbook will generate interest in finding more ways to establish an atmosphere of cooperation and support in any group of people, whether children or adults. Please let us know of new things you are trying out and finding successful.

Games can also be used by adults as learning tools. For example, Bill Bauer, who has done work with church youth activities in India, has put together an intriguing sequence of games and questions which can't help but lead into a thoughtful discussion on attitudes toward values, such as competition and success. Here is a description of that process:

Bill Bauer introduced the topic by asking the question, "What is social responsibility?" and giving 10 minutes for each participant to write his or her own definition. The issues of competition and cooperation were then explored by playing the following games:

1) Candy Eat (invented by Bill Bauer): "The group was divided into teams of three. One by one each team was directed to a piece of unwrapped, hard candy suspended from a string about 12" above the tallest person in the group. The group of three was told that they might have one piece of candy if they could get it down without touching the string or candy with their hands. The only way to get the candy was for two team members to lift the third and the third take the candy in his or her mouth.

After taking it in his or her mouth, the only thing to do was for that person to eat the candy while the other two did without. There was only enough candy for one person per group.

2) Musical Chairs
3) Musical Laps (see p. 16)

Musical Laps (see p. 16)

We then divided into small groups of 6 to 8 persons to discuss:

a. What were the differences in the games?
b. Which did you most enjoy and why?
c. What kinds of players are required for success in each game?
d. Of the different types of players, which best expressed your individual nature. Why?
e. List games you know according to which of the three types they most represent.

Many good points came out of the discussion, and values were further reinforced. The enjoyment of many for the first game, even if they did not get the candy, led to the further question, 'Who really got the greatest "prize" in the first game?' "

123

Name games

Name games help us to learn each other's names. Oftentimes when a group is meeting for the first time, an active name game will provide a positive affirmative tone and ease the tension of being with new people. It's helpful to realize that people can help each other remember names, that there is nothing wrong with not knowing everyone's name. We hope these games will ease that embarrassment and create the kind of atmosphere where it will be easier to remember. An example is to have people, in turn, tell their names, and an animal they would like to be, mythical or real.

GESTURE NAME GAME

Circle. This game is physically active and a lot of fun. The person initiating the game needs to encourage spontaneity and keep the pace lively and quick. Each person in turn, without thinking, makes a gesture while saying her or his name at the same time. Name and gesture go together in some sort of rhythm (for example, Bob Jacobs: while saying "Bob," he raises his hand; "Jacobs," stamps his foot on the first syllable and then his other foot on the second syllable). Then the group together repeats the name and gesture twice. The second person now takes a turn. A visual, non-verbal impression of a person along with his or her name will help to associate names and faces.

HICKEY PICKEY HOKEY POKEY DOO DAD

Circle. One person in the center points a finger at another and says, "Hickey pickey hokey pokey doo dad." Before the phrase is finished, the person pointed at must call out the name of the person to the right. If the name is not called out quickly enough, the speaker moves into the center. In a large group, several persons may be in the center. Keep the game moving quickly.

In case you're wondering...

We have consciously and consistently avoided calling anyone "It." The word "it" is an impersonal pronoun which carries a lot of connotations and past feelings about games. We say instead, "the center person," "the leader," "who wants to go first?" etc.

"ARE YOU   ?"

When people are first coming into the room, the leader suggests that they walk around getting to know each other and write the names of everyone on individual slips of paper. Then at some point in the meeting when things need livening up, everyone passes out the slips of paper to the people whose names are on them. This is an enjoyable way to associate faces with names.

JACK-IN-THE-BOX NAME GAME

Circle. First person starts by standing up and saying her name: "I'm Cynthia." Then she introduces four people on her left, starting with the farthest person: "This is Joe, Susan, Pam, Bob." When each name is said, that person stands up and sits down quickly. There is a jack-in-the-box effect, people standing and sitting one after the other. Then the person on Cynthia's right stands up and introduces himself and the four people to his left: "I'm Pat and this is Susan, Pam, Bob and Cynthia," dropping one person introduced previously (in this case, Joe). Again, when each person's name is mentioned, he or she stands or sits quickly. By the time introductions get around the circle, the names will be more familiar and the smiles a little bigger.

With younger children, fewer people can be introduced, maybe one or two.

THE ITCH NAME GAME
(from Jonathan Freedman)

A good name game. First person says, "My name is Joan and I itch here" (scratching some part of the body, e.g., head). Second person says, "Her name is Joan and she itches there" (reaching out to scratch Joan on the head) "and my name is Jim and I itch here" (scratching). Third person says, "His name is Jim and he itches there and my name is Marcia and I itch here" (scratching the other person and then herself). And so it continues around the circle amidst the giggles.

QUALITY INITIALS (learned from Ann Lenhart)

To start a group meeting positively, each person thinks about the two or three initials of her or his name (e.g., Ellen Deacon would take "E" and "D") and finds two affirming qualities that describe himself or herself (in Ellen's case, "elegant and dynamic"). The beauty of this activity is that it gives people a chance to think about themselves in an affirming way.

In case you're wondering...

The six headings (Name Games, Opening-up Activities, etc.) show the purposes of the games and the uses to which they may be put. However, in some cases we had to be arbitrary. An example is Touch Blue (under Opening-up Activities), which is simultaneously an "opening-up," a "touching," and an "attention-out" activity. Thoughtful, sensitive adults will know when and for what purpose these activities are to be used.

125

Opening-up activities

These activities are particularly helpful in new groups, where something active gets people inter-acting with one another on a light, non-threatening note. Touch Blue has been especially useful, and has been used over and over again as an opener. It is also possible to use it as a gentle way of reaching out. If people are not playing, it may be an indication of their feeling about the group. In this case, one may say, "Touch blue on all those who are not playing," creating an easy opportunity for people to focus for a minute on those not participating, for whatever reason.

BUMP
(Jill Wilsher, Speech and Drama Center, England)

Music needed; any number of players; large space. When the music starts, all walk around very fast in all directions, deliberately bumping GENTLY into as many others as possible.

Music stops: Each participant links arms with the nearest person, and they exchange first names.

Music starts: Remaining in linked pairs, they continue to go around the room, this time avoiding bumps, but talking non-stop to their partners.

Music stops: the pairs separate. Each person now grabs *two* other people, who link arms and introduce themselves.

Music starts: Groups continue to walk around and talk.

From now on, each time the music stops the leader calls a different number, and the groups form and re-form accordingly. When the leader feels that everyone has met everyone else, she or he can start making the groups bigger and bigger until the whole group is trying to walk, linked noisily together.

Variation: With young children, simply use the music's stopping as the time to give a new instruction (e.g., walk around shaking people's hands/hugging them/touching their right feet/bumping into them while walking backwards).

MEETINGS
(Jill Wilsher, Speech and Drama Center, England)

Music needed; any number of players; large space. When the music starts, players walk around quickly in all directions, avoiding contact. When the music stops, each player shakes hands with the nearest person and discovers as much personal information as possible until the music restarts (5-7 seconds). The process is repeated; each time the child must greet someone new. The game continues until all have met. *Note:* keep it moving.

TOUCH BLUE
The leader announces, "Everyone touch blue!" (or another color, object,' etc.) Participants must touch something on another person. "Touch a sandal!" or "Touch a bracelet!" ensures physical contact. There are endless variations, such as "Touch a knee with your left thumb!" Dorothy Flanagan, a teacher of second and third graders, found it particularly helpful to do this activity in slow motion. Her children liked moving v-e-r-r-ry slowly.

Physical contact games

Recall the child who sits on your lap, the spontaneous hug, the sitting close while reading a story, the holding hands while walking down the street? Children have a natural sense of physically separating and connecting to others. This ability to reach out and touch others in a free, giving manner is one of the most endearing qualities that children possess. The teacher who is openly and warmly affectionate with young children always has them in his or her lap. This kind of warm human contact helps to create a safe, supportive environment.

However, it seems that the older we get, the less likely we are to feel and act on those natural impulses of reaching out to others. We somehow learn, "It's not the thing to do," "It's silly," or it means you're "in love with someone." Or if it's a boy, it might mean he is a "sissy." Linking arms can be suspect. Inhibitions, acute embarrassment, and fear of being ridiculed are the barriers which keep us all from caring about and supporting one another.

As a result, many of our games have been chosen in order to break down this embarrassment. A good way to do this is to set up situations where people can laugh it off. It becomes acceptable and non-threatening to touch another person within the context and limits of the game. For instance, Touch Blue (see games) is a light, enjoyable activity which encourages touching: a shoe, a bracelet, an ear, etc. Another example is Musical Laps. Afterwards one feels more open and friendly. Laughter relaxes, and consequently frees people to be more aware of others.

SWAT

A rolled-up newspaper is placed on a chair in the center of a circle of chairs. There must be enough chairs for everyone. Whoever starts (Person A), picks up the rolled newspaper and lightly hits a seated person (Person B) on the legs, quickly places the newspaper on the chair in the center and sits down in his or her own seat. Person B tries to pick up the newspaper from the chair and hit Person A on the legs before Person A can get back to his or her seat. If Person A is hit by Person B, Person A remains in the center. If not, Person B becomes Center Person. Should the swatter put the rolled newspaper on the chair in such a way that it falls off, he or she must put it back on the chair before sitting down.

Note: People should be encouraged to swat rapidly and not contemplate. The leader can remind people often to hit on the leg area only. Hitting hard is not the object.

SARDINES

One person goes and hides. After a suitable interval, the rest go to find the hider. When someone finds the hider, he or she hides alongside and keeps quiet until everyone is hiding in the same place. The first finder becomes hider next time. Fun in the dark!

VEGETABLE CART

People sit in a circle with one person in the center. People by pairs choose a vegetable. Center Person calls the names of one or more vegetables. Those persons whose vegetable was called must get up and switch chairs, while Center Person also tries to grab one of the two vacant chairs. The person who wasn't able to get a chair goes to the center and the game continues. If Center Person calls "Vegetable Cart," then everyone changes seats. With twenty or more people, each group of four is one vegetable. Caution: strong, sturdy chairs and lots of room are needed.

Variation: If a class is learning the names of the states, students could pair up by states, and all would move when the Center Person called "United States."

HA HA

Lots of floor space needed, or a lawn under a warm sun. Someone lies down and the next person lies down putting his or her head on the stomach of the first person. The third person puts his or her head on the stomach of the second person, and so on. Then the first person says HA! Second person: HA HA! Third person: HA HA HA! and so on, increasing the number of HA's. The laughter is infectious. Try it and see how it feels.

127

SWITCHBACKS (variation on Musical Laps)

Everyone is in pairs, back to back. If there is an odd number of people, the free person sings or talks in monologue (or plays some kind of simple instrument, e.g. drum), while everyone moves around the room or field, back-to-back with his or her partner (elbows can be locked). When the singing stops, each person finds a new partner and the free person must find a partner. The current odd person is now the music-maker and the game is repeated. If there are an even number of people, there is no free person, and someone is designated as the caller while he or she participates.

Variation: Each time the music stops, the music-maker can quickly indicate a different part of the body that is to be touched (head-to-head or big-toe-to-big-toe).

DRAGON

Works best with not more than seven adults, or not more than seven to eight children. Everyone gets into a line holding the waist of the person in front with their hands, not arms. Then the "head" (first person in line) of the dragon tries to touch the "tail" (the last person in line) while the "body" (people in between) help keep the "tail" from being touched without anyone losing grip of the waist of the person in front. If there is more than one line, then each line can operate independently of each other *or* think up something that would cause the various lines to interact.

LEAP FROG

You know how this one goes!

In case you're wondering...

The Nonviolence and Children Program has decided to avoid as sexist the exclusive use of the masculine pronoun. Although "he or she," "his or her," etc., may be more cumbersome, we feel it is important to extend our growing consciousness into the written form.

128

EIN ZWEI PIP EINMAL [Eye-n Zv-eye Pe-e-ep Eye-n Mah-l]

This game works best with a group that has been together for some time. It starts with a circle with one less chair than there are people. Someone starts in the center. The Center Person closes his or her eyes and everyone changes seats. The Center Person, with eyes closed, sits down on someone's lap and says, "Ein Zwei Pip Einmal" (one two peep once more) and the person whose lap is sat on has to say "peep" (with a disguised voice). The Center Person tries to guess the identity of the peeper and has three chances to ask "Ein Zwei..." in order to guess. Whether the Center Person guesses right or not, a new Center Person is chosen and the game starts over.

THIS IS A HUG. A WHAT?

Sit in a circle. Person A says to Person B on the right, "This is a hug," and hugs Person B. Person B says, "A what?" to which Person A responds, "A hug," again demonstrating. Person B then says to the person on the right (Person C), "This is a hug," hugging Person C, who asks, "A what?" Person B asks "A what?" to Person A, to which Person A responds, "A hug," hugging Person B. Person B turns and says, "A hug," hugging Person C. And so on. The question, "A what?" is relayed back to Person A, and the answer (a hug) is sent back to the individual.

In the meantime, Person A says to the person on the *left,* "This is a handshake," shaking hands with that person, who asks, "A what?" Person A responds, "A handshake," and on around the circle. When the hugs and handshakes (or any form of physical affection) meet on the other side of the circle, it gets hilarious!

I'M GOING ON A TRIP

"I'm going to _____" (whoever has a turn gets to choose where) "and I'm taking a hug," says the person who is first, while sensitively demonstrating with the person to the right (Person B) in the circle. Person B then says, "I'm going on a trip to _____ and I'm taking a hug" (demonstrating with Person C) "and a pat on the back" (again demonstrating with Person C). Person C takes these two things and adds one more, demonstrating all of them on Person D, and so on around, using expressions of physical affection. If people forget, it's fun to remind them.

Variation: People take along something they like about themselves.

Cooperative games

It's important to set a tone, to have fun and to emphasize that there is no winner or loser. When children have a hard time remembering something in a game, give them some space and then allow others to help them. If a person gets frustrated with being the Center Person, have someone else take the center. Some games such as Musical Laps have been adapted from the old ones we've known since childhood. The whole group learns to be together in play, thereby increasing the links between people.

ANIMAL SOUNDS
(Penni and Brooks Eldredge-Martin)

Room darkened; eyes closed; one large ball. Everyone sits in a circle and people in turn select and mimic different animal sounds as their own personal signals. The initiator of the game makes her or his sound and then the sound of the "animal" to which she or he intends to roll the ball. The "animal" whose sound is made replies (to help initiator direct the ball). The initiator then rolls the ball toward the intended animal. If that animal receives the ball, she or he responds with her or his sound and the animals show happiness by making all their sounds in unison (this also reminds others what animals are present). If the initiator misses the intended animal, the animal that receives the ball returns it to the initiator after making her or his sound.

SLIP THE DISC
(Penni and Brooks Eldredge-Martin)

Everyone forms a circle, kneeling on hands and knees with heads facing inward. An object, e.g. a 4" diameter circular piece of cork, or a Frisbee, is placed upon one person's back. The object of the game is to pass the cork successfully from back to back around the circle without the use of hands. If it falls, it is replaced (by hand) on the back of the last person who had it.

HUMAN PRETZEL

Two people leave the room. The others hold hands in a circle and twist themselves over and under and through each other without dropping hands. The two people waiting outside come back in and are challenged to untangle the group. The Pretzel cooperates as the "untanglers" figure out who goes where.

PRU-EE (learned from Bernard De Koven)

A delightful activity for large groups (15 or more). All eyes should be closed. The leader whispers in someone's ear, "You're the PRU-EE." Now everyone, including the PRU-EE, begins to mingle with eyes shut. Each person is to find another's hand, shake it and ask, "Pru-ee?" If the other person also asks, "Pru-ee?" they drop hands and go on to someone else. Everyone goes around asking except for the PRU-EE, who remains silent the whole time. When a person gets no response to the question, "Pru-ee?" he or she knows the PRU-EE is found, hangs onto that hand, and becomes part of the PRU-EE, also remaining silent. Anyone shaking hands with the PRU-EE (now two people) becomes a part of it, making it larger and larger. If someone finds only clasped hands and silence, he or she can join the line at that point. Soon the cries of "Pru-ee?" will dwindle, and the PRU-EE will increase until everyone in the room is holding hands. Then the leader asks for eyes to be opened. There are always gasps of surprise and laughter. *Note:* The "pru-ee?" sounds like a high-pitched little bird call.

SINGING SYLLABLE

All sit in a circle. One person goes out of the room. The rest of the group picks one word with three or more syllables, e.g., *No vem ber*. Count off by syllables so that each person has a syllable. Then pick a simple song, such as "Row, Row, Row Your Boat." Each person sings his or her syllable to the tune of the song. For example, one would sing "no, no, no, no," etc., and another person would sing "vem, vem, vem," etc., to the same tune, and so on. Then the volunteer would come back into the room and try to put the different syllables together and identify the word.

129

RAINSTORM

One person acts as the conductor of the storm and stands in the center of the circle. As with an orchestra, the conductor brings each person into the storm (symphony) in turn. Standing in front of one person, the conductor starts rubbing her or his own hands together. The person imitates the motion. The conductor turns around slowly in place until everyone is rubbing hands together. Then, coming around to the first person again, and while everyone is still rubbing hands, he or she starts snapping fingers. This motion also goes all the way around, with each person continuing the first motion until getting a new direction from the conductor. The game goes on with hands slapping thighs and finally with both slapping of thighs and stamping of feet—the crescendo of the storm. As with a thundershower, the volume decreases as the conductor goes through the above steps in reverse order until the last person rubbing hands is silent.

BLIND NEIGHBOR

Works best if people know each other well. Chairs in a circle, one for each person. Half of the group sits down, with alternating vacant chairs. They shut their eyes. The other people then take the vacant chairs and start singing, perhaps each singing a different song. Each shut-eyed person tries to guess who is sitting to the right. If the singing together makes it too difficult for the shut-eyed people to guess, then the open-eyed people should sing one at a time. After the guessing, reverse roles and start over.

WATER CUP PASS

Everyone stands in a circle with a paper cup in his or her teeth. One person's cup is filled with water. That person begins by pouring the water into the next person's cup without hands, and so on around the circle. A delightful game on a hot summer day.

ELEPHANT-PALM TREE

All stand in a circle. The one in the center points to a person and says either "elephant" or "palm tree." To make an elephant, the person pointed to bends at the waist and clasps hands and swings arms like an elephant's trunk. The two people on each side stretch both arms over the "trunk" person, imitating an elephant ear. All three of these gestures must happen at the SAME TIME.

To make a palm tree, the person pointed to stands tall with hands clasped together and straight up above his or her head. Persons on each side make fronds by holding up the outside arm away from the middle person and pointing it away from the body.

If someone makes a mistake or hesitates a fraction too long, then the center person of the threesome must go into the center to point to others. It's a very funny, successful game, and people don't mind making mistakes because everyone is laughing so much. With very small children, teachers have found it better to do one at a time—to teach the elephant first and have them practice it for several weeks before introducing the palm tree gesture.

Variations:

Gorilla—middle person makes a gorilla face and grunts and swings arms, two side people scratch the sides of middle person.

1776—center person acts as if he or she is holding a flag standard, the person on the right as if drumming a drum, the person on the left as if holding and playing a flute.

Students will love making up new ones.

Note: in large groups, the game will flow more if there are several people in the center.

NONVERBAL BIRTHDAY LINE-UP

This is a challenging cooperative activity. The leader gives only these directions: "Without talking, line yourselves up according to the month and day you were born. The idea is to have us all in a line from January to December." The participants themselves must figure out *how* they can communicate without words and *where* they should start and end the line. *Note:* It's reassuring to hear that it doesn't matter if everyone is not placed perfectly in line. The point of this activity is to work together.

PASS THE SHOE

Due to copyright and time problems, this outstanding, lively and cooperative song-activity could not be printed here. However, it is well worth the time to locate the *Fireside Book of Children's Songs* by Marie Winn (New York: Simon and Schuster, 1966, p. 173). Our suggested adaptation is that the participants pass the shoes on the down beats of *each measure,* not just measures 1, 3 and 5. The song has to be sung very slowly at first, so that the sense of rhythm is established, but soon the leader can gradually increase the tempo. The shoes will probably end up in one big pile with everyone laughing!

ALPHABET

This is a good activity for getting people moving and interacting (works best with more than 10 people). Each person is to be a letter, either by assignment or by choice. Then everyone is to seek out other letters to form words.

Variation: limit the words to a specific theme, size, etc. What others can you think of?

TOUCHBEE (Cooperative Frisbee) •

An interesting variation on simply throwing the Frisbee(s) back and forth with a group of six to eight people is that the person catching the Frisbee must be touched by or touching another person while receiving the Frisbee. People become more involved and aware of each other when they anticipate dashing over to touch the catcher. Even more interest will be added if two or three Frisbees are thrown simultaneously.

KNOTS

(a variation on Pretzel learned from Eric Bachman)

Everyone closes eyes and moves together, each person taking another person's hand in each of his or her hands. When each person has two hands, then all open their eyes and try to untangle themselves without dropping hands. The group must work together to get out the knots. It leads to very amusing situations because although the group may end up in one big circle, most of the time there will be a knot or two in the circle, and even two or more circles, either intertwined or separate. It's great fun and leads to group cooperation.

LAP BALL

Everyone sits on the floor in a circle (7 to 15 people can fit). Legs are extended in front and all feet are in the center. (If an old tire were placed in the center, more people could play.) Hands support the body by being placed behind it on the floor. Heels are not to be lifted and the hands must stay behind the back, though they can move. The object is to keep the ball off the ground while passing it quickly from lap to lap. If it gets stuck around the ankles, people can think up a creative way to get it moving again. The fun increases when two balls are being passed simultaneously in different directions. The cooperative aspect of the game is evident when two people are working together to keep the ball from falling between them on the floor.

Light plastic balls work best.

RHYTHM CLAP

Good for large groups (10 or more). Everyone closes eyes and begins to clap or beat any rhythm he or she chooses. At first, it will sound disjointed and chaotic, but gradually people try to change in order to create a fine rhythmical experience. It can end at any time by people opening eyes or by slowing down the rhythm. People who believe themselves to be without rhythm will feel pleased with this activity.

HERMAN-HENRIETTA

Herman-Henrietta is an imaginary magical blob of clay. Anyone can shape it into anything—anything! The teacher begins to pantomime pulling the magical blob from his or her pocket and sets the tone by getting involved with creating something. To start with, it's helpful to create things that the children (or adults) can easily identify. It's fun to guess what's being made, but not necessary, as it is essentially a nonverbal game. Then the magical lump is mushed down to its original size (still in pantomime) and passed reverently to the next person. The game continues around the circle.

MUSICAL LAPS (Sandra Cangiano at an Abington Friends School faculty workshop)

This is a cooperative version of Musical Chairs. The whole group forms a circle, all facing in one direction, close together, each with hands on the waist of the person ahead. When the music starts, everyone begins to walk forward. When the music stops, everyone sits down in the lap of the person to the rear. If the whole group succeeds in sitting in laps without anyone falling to the floor, the *group* wins. If people fall down, *gravity* wins. Works best with more than ten people about the same size (a big man will have a hard time sitting in the lap of a six year old!).

ACTIVE NOISE (Physical activity)

All stand. Leader begins an activity and noise and everyone follows (e.g., spreads arms wide and sings a syllable—repeats motion over and over quickly). Then leader initiates another activity and sound over the noise of the first, and everyone then imitates the second activity. At this point, everyone should have the idea, and anyone with an idea can initiate a group motion and noise, which is then imitated by all the others. A new activity should not be started until the previous one has been taken up by the whole group.

BARNYARD

People stand in a large circle, choose six animals (less for a group smaller than 20) and count off by animals; or a slip of paper with the name of an animal on it is passed out to each person. Then, with everyone's eyes closed (or a dark room could be used), each person finds all the others of his or her kind by constantly calling the animal sounds, "Baa-a-a," "Meow, meow," etc. When two of the same animals come across each other, they hold hands and find others until they are all together. It is a very funny game! *Note:* The idea is *not* to finish first, but merely to find your own kind.

"I think we need to remember that each of us has particular strengths and weaknesses. In that sense we are not all equal. The better we realize these real strengths and weaknesses, the more easily we can guard against some of the stereotyped and imagined ones that society creates. I like to think of the Musical Laps game as an analogy. When everyone works together we each sit on the lap of the person behind us. There is no one on top and one one on the bottom. I think this is like people and their talents. We are each better than others in some things, and others are better than we are in other areas. When we all can work together, we become as effective as the sum of our best talents. I think we should be striving toward this ideal working-together situation. We should be trying to develop our real strengths and to help others develop their real strengths."
—*Hal Taylor, a Nonviolence and Children subcommittee member*

BODY SCULPTURE

Teachers are discovering body sculpture to be a naturally cooperative activity and an excellent means of encouraging group participation. It is also an opportunity to become aware of and to explore the use of space.

An exciting aspect of this activity is that people of all ages can participate. For instance, at a recent family workshop we asked each family to make an abstract sculpture, first demonstrating how it might happen. We suggested that the youngest member of each family shape her or his family into a design or sculpture. Children as young as three or four seemed to enjoy this opportunity. For one four-year-old girl it was the first time she had been in a position of giving the orders in her family. She loved it so much that she was in a good mood all day!

Mirroring as a pre-sculpturing experience has been used with very young children. The teacher stands in front of the group and slowly moves, encouraging the children to try to follow the movements. Each child could have a chance to be leader. Another possibility is to divide into pairs and ask the group to watch each pair in turn, trying to guess which person is the leader and which is the follower.

Building one body sculpture on top of another is an interesting way to use space and work cooperatively. The facilitator divides the participants into two groups and asks Group A to leave the room. Group B designs itself into a body sculpture. Group A now comes in and appreciates what has been made. Its task is to create a body sculpture within and around the one already formed, without touching anyone in Group B. When Group A has formed itself, Group B disengages, again without touching the other group, and stands back to look at the spaces created by its departure. This process can be repeated three or four times. Participants seem to enjoy observing a creation as well as being involved in it.

CLAPPING GAME

One person goes out of the room. The rest of the group decides on an object for the person to find, or an action for the person to do. The person returns to try to find the object while the group claps. The group will help the person complete the task by clapping louder and louder as the person approaches the object or act decided upon. If the person is far away from doing the activity or finding the object, the clapping is soft.

Variation: This game can also be played with two people going out of the room and coming back to do something in tandem. Examples of things to have people do: hug each other, face each other with hands on shoulders, sit back-to-back. Think up your own variations!

A highlight for me of the Nonviolence and Children Program's work at the Children's School took place on the beautiful April morning when we all went outside to make body sculptures. Following directions, each child found a partner with whom to make a little two-body sculpture. One at a time the pairs were connected, creating a big group sculpture. I wish I had had my camera. Next the children were asked to move away from the large sculpture with their original partners and take a few minutes to tell each other "something you liked about doing a sculpture with the other person." Almost at once every pair of children was sitting on the ground and talking. It didn't matter that I couldn't hear a word they said; just watching gave me an incredibly warm feeling, and it wasn't coming just from the sunshine.

—*Karen Zaur*

133

THUMB STORY (learned from Barbara Gottesman)

Good in small groups. In turn, each person holds up a thumb and tells an outright lie about that thumb. For example, "This thumb saved Holland by being plugged into the dike."

ONE WORD STORY

Circle. Each person in turn says one word which will add to the story that is developing. For instance, "I...saw...a...monster...in...the...lemon...soup..." and so forth. Very funny! Works best when the pace is lively.

REFLECTIVE LISTENING STORY TELLING

Everyone is sitting in a circle. Someone starts a story. The teacher sets the tone by starting with something he or she knows would catch the group's interest, stopping at some dramatic moment. The next person to the left (or right) takes over the story. Encourage short and lively accounts.

ELBOW-NOSE

Circle. Good for small groups. Leader starts by turning to the person on the right and *saying,* "This is my *elbow*" while *pointing* to his or her *nose*. This second person then responds, "This is my nose" while pointing to his or her own elbow. Then the second person turns to the next person on the right (third person) and points to some part of the body while naming another part, to which the third person responds with the opposite, and so on. Pace needs to be quick and lively, otherwise it tends to drag.

TIN MAN

(Penni and Brooks Eldredge-Martin—see p. 22)

The object is to give everyone in a darkened room a heart made of felt or construction paper. All eyes remain closed until the end of the game. Participants give one of two sound signals, "lub" or "dub." If someone has a heart to give, he or she says "dub." If someone needs a heart, the sound is "lub." The only rule is that two participants cannot exchange hearts; that is, one cannot receive a heart from the person it came from (this prevents the game from ending the moment it starts).

Variation: People write heart-felt wishes on the hearts and, at the end of the game, share them with each other.

ZOOM

First person quickly says "Zoom" with a turn of the head to the person next to him or her, who passes it on to the next person, who passes it on to the next person, and so on around the circle, until someone responds with "Zerk!" in which case "Zoom!" goes around the circle in the opposite direction. If too many "Zerks" keep "Zoom" from going around the circle enough, someone can say "Nefrigliani!" in which case it has to "Zoom" all the way around the circle before "Zerk" is permitted again.

Variation: When saying "Zoom," people stand up, raise arms, or add any gesture to the words.

LET'S BUILD A MACHINE

People try to represent a machine with each person portraying a moving part. The machine can be imaginary, allowing for creativity in the wheres and hows of moving parts. Or it can be a real machine (washing machine, sewing machine, school machine theme) in which the fun lies in trying to figure out how to represent the parts with people. This game is good in the physical contact as well as the cooperation category.

Note: "Machine" is good for the physically handicapped, who can use crutches, etc. A person confined to a wheelchair can be of central importance. Good for social studies units, e.g. Iroquois Indian machine.

Values clarification activities

There are many good books on values clarification; however, we recommend Simon, Howe and Kirschenbaum's book Values Clarification: Handbook of Practical Strategies. *To summarize some of our insights about this area: a value for an individual is something he or she has chosen freely from alternatives, affirmed publicly and acted upon. Things that seem to muddle the choosing of values are the lack of information about alternatives, and feelings, such as fear of the judgment of others, not being liked, etc. Games can provide a safe, non-competitive place for children to start choosing and reflecting upon what values they want to hold and to explore the feelings that get in the way of free choice.*

SUE'S GAME (Susanne Gowan)

Everyone takes a paper and pencil and fills in the blanks in these sentences:

If I were a color, I'd be _____ .
If I were an animal, I'd be _____ .
If I were a fabric, I'd be _____ .
If I were an athlete, I'd be _____ .

What others can you think of?

Group leader then collects the papers and reads them anonymously, having people guess who wrote what.

CORNERS GAME*

The purpose of this game is to have people begin to choose and talk about their values. The teacher names two items and designates a corner of the room for each one. Each person then chooses the item he or she feels closest to and goes to that corner of the room. The leader suggests that people pair up with one other person in their corner and describe the reasons why they have chosen that item. After a couple of minutes, the group leader assigns another item to each corner, and people again choose by walking to that corner and describing their reasons for choosing.

Depending on the age, and the kinds of things the teachers want to focus on, some possible combinations might be: a dandelion or an orchid? a patchwork quilt or an electric blanket (a unit on energy-saving devices)? ocean or mountains (geography)? a book or a movie? being blind or being deaf? Indian Chief or Queen?

JUNGLE WALK

(adapted from the Corners Game)

Children pretend that they are one of four people walking through the jungle. They can be the first, second, third or last in line, choosing the position they think they would prefer. The leader designates four corners or areas of the room, one for each position, for participants to walk to once they have made their choice. Discussion ensues in each corner.

Note: for first and second graders, the teacher can simply pick opposites or similar things, and children can move to one side of the room and back, without explaining why. Red or blue? night or day? chocolate or vanilla? The combination of choosing and moving from one side to the other creates an exciting activity for them. They also enjoy thinking up the two items and suggesting them to the group.

Variation: As people finish describing reasons to another person in the same corner, ask that someone from the "ocean" corner explain why he or she chose ocean over mountains, and then the same from the "mountains" corner. Comments such as "mine is better than yours" or any development of defending or arguing one's viewpoint should be firmly discouraged. The idea is simply to share and explore without put-downs from others.

*Rephrased from "Either-or Forced Choice," *Values Clarification: A Handbook of Practical Strategies for Teachers and Students,* by Sidney B. Simon, Leland W. Howe and Howard Kirschenbaum. New York: Hart Publishing Co., Inc., 1972. Used by permission.

135

Attention-out activities

Attention-out activities are light quick games to help young people change their focus or **attention** from preoccupation or day-dreaming **out** to what's happening in the room here and now. The learning processes are slowed down by many of the feelings children carry with them from home, from the interactions in the hallways, or from the playground. Where some children tend to get angry and lash out, others might cry or simply withdraw into themselves. Any person who is absorbed with feelings doesn't have much attention left to take in the information and skills being communicated by the teacher. As adults, we know how hard it is to keep our mind on the driving or on our job when we've had a spat at home with our loved ones. So it is with our children.

What we are discovering is that these games, particularly the attention-out activities, tend to bring attention back into the classroom away from the hurts and daydreaming. While a classroom teacher cannot be responsible for all those feelings, there are ways to help people function more effectively. For example, a teacher, noticing the children's attention wandering some warm afternoon, might suggest that the class sing "My Bonnie Lies Over the Ocean" (see games) for several minutes. Everyone then can turn back to the work refreshed. Or perhaps the young people can stand up, walk around and shake hands with five other peers, and then sit down again. And so on.... These quick one-minute activities are purposely created in order to clear the mind of any fogginess, and to bring the focus back into the room and onto the task at hand.

The same activities can be applied to business or faculty meetings. Many times, we become so intent on our discussions and decision-making that we get a little "heavy" or "bogged down." Why not try a couple of attention-out games? The laughter will help clear the mind and provide a lighter tone to the meeting.

ATTENTION-OUT SONGS

HEAD, SHOULDERS, KNEES AND TOES

To the tune of "There's a Tavern in the Town," everyone sings

Head and shoulders, knees and toes, knees and toes
Head and shoulders, knees and toes, knees and toes
Eyes and ears and mouth and nose
Head and shoulders, knees and toes, knees and toes.

The song is sung through the first time with each person touching each body part mentioned as the group sings the song. The second time the song is sung, everyone omits singing "head," but the hands still touch the head; the rest of the song is sung as usual, with gestures. Then, the third time, "head and shoulders" is omitted, but gestures continue. By the time the activity is ended, people are "singing" the song silently, with the gestures substituting for the words.

Morning in the Jungle. Each individual chooses a jungle animal. Then everyone closes eyes and pretends that dawn is coming and that the animals are beginning to wake up. Softly at first, everyone together makes the sound of the chosen animal and gradually increases the volume until it is very loud. It's great!

136

MY BONNIE LIES OVER THE OCEAN

Everyone sings this song, and wherever a word starting with "b" is sung, people stand if sitting, or sit if standing.

My bonnie *(stand)* lies over the ocean
My bonnie *(sit)* lies over the sea
My bonnie *(stand)* lies over the ocean
Oh, bring *(sit)* back *(stand)* my bonnie *(sit)* to me, to me
Bring *(stand)* back *(sit)*
Bring *(stand)* back *(sit)*
Oh, bring *(stand)* back *(sit)* my bonnie *(stand)* to me, to me
Bring *(sit)* back *(stand)*
Bring *(sit)* back *(stand)*
Oh, bring *(sit)* back *(stand)* my bonnie *(sit)* to me.

Variation: Every alternate person stands up before the song begins. Then, as everyone sings, the standing people will start the sequence by sitting, and the sitting people will start by standing. A jack-in-the-box effect and confusion will add to the fun! Or, in a circle, people place their hands (gently) on the heads of the persons on each side and then on their own heads.

QUICK ONE-MINUTE ACTIVITIES

Stand up, grasp both ears and walk around making the sound of your favorite animal to several other people you meet, and sit down again.

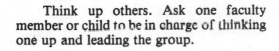

Think up others. Ask one faculty member or child to be in charge of thinking one up and leading the group.

Say, "Make your face as big as you can, as wide and tall as possible." Then say, "Make your face as small and teensy-tiny as you can." Of course, take a look around the table or room!

Stand up, touch your left knee with your right hand, your right hip with your left hand, and cluck like a chicken, then sit down again.

Stand up, shake hands with four other people, singing Yankee Doodle, and sit down again in a different chair.

Each person in turn shares his or her mother's maiden name.

137

Inventing one's own games

Most of our lives, we look to others for ideas and instruction; as children, to the parent or teacher figure, later to the institutional or bureaucratic authority. We are so used to following others or going to a book to get ideas that it is hard to feel confident in our own ability to create something on our own. It's a bit unnerving even to consider creating something brand-new like a game. "Who, me? Create a game? I couldn't do that!" says the mind. But the fact is that any one of us is capable of innovating, if given the opportunity and encouragement.

For instance, two teachers, Penni and Brooks Eldredge-Martin, were leading a workshop on affirmation and cooperative games for the parents of children attending the Barclay School in Pennsylvania. Brooks described a time in class when younger and older children were playing the traditional game of Musical Chairs together. The younger children had ended up crying, the older ones became very angry, and the parents had stepped in to console both. This led the Barclay parents into a lively discussion about changing traditional games into cooperative ones. Someone suggested Pin-the-tail-on-the-donkey as an example of an awkward social game in which one person is blindfolded while everyone else watches. No one helps, there is no like-minded goal, it is simply a watch-and-laugh game at the expense of the blindfoldee.

When asked to throw out ideas, someone connected "Pin" with the Tin Man of the Wizard of Oz, and another said, "How about giving the Tin Man a heart?" With growing interest, people began to question and suggest. "How could we alleviate the problem of no common goal?" Some remembered Pru-ee (p. 13) and the reasons why it was so well-liked. There was a common goal; being in the dark made it safe; no person had to stand around being watched like an object. Gradually, ideas being added and discarded, an activity evolved where people gave hearts to one another, in the dark. Someone chimed in with, "You've got to let people know," which led to chanting sounds of "lub" and "dub" filling the room while people gave and received paper hearts (see game for complete details).

The evening continued with growing excitement as several other games were created. The comments at the end of the two-hour workshop were, "Why stop?" "We could go on all night!" How sad it is that we have become so "adult," that we have so few opportunities really to let the childlike playfulness within all of us emerge and flow spontaneously.

138

Invent...create...adapt

One way to invent a game is to start with a small group, throwing out ideas, discarding, changing, adapting until something comes up that is fun to play. Then share it with another group, to see whether it works.

At a games workshop that I was co-leading last year in West Philadelphia, I was nervously encouraging the participants to create a game or activity. I was excited, hopeful about the outcome, but my head was questioning, "What if this doesn't work?" I had suggested we break into two small groups of 5 or 6, work within a time limit of 10 minutes, and come up with a game. When we came back together to share, the first group had us all sit on the floor in a row with outstretched legs. We were to pass a ball from lap to lap without hands. Spontaneously someone from the second group suggested sitting in a circle, and "Lap Ball" came into being. None of us had ever created a game before, and we all felt terribly proud of ourselves. What's more, Lap Ball has become a resounding success!

—*Marta Harrison*

Others invent, too

At a training session last year, a group of dynamic young, inner-city camp counselors made up a "cooling" game for those hot summer days, calling it "Water Cup Pass." They, too, felt proud and were excited about inventing their own game for their campers.

You can do it, too!

Catch a Falling Star

Because Marta is a lover of games, we wanted to give her one at her going-away party. I volunteered to make it up, even though my only thought on leaving the brainstorming session was that Marta and star sound nice together. Not much of a start!

Soon I was humming the song "Catch a Falling Star" and wondering how one person could catch a Marta star and put it not just in her own pocket, but in everybody's. But what would be the star: a secret? a shiny object? a special handshake? They all might make someone feel excluded.

It was the day of the party and still the "stars" had not come out. Karen was to compose a round for Marta, so we met for lunch in the park to help each other out. Who knows what might have happened if the balloon man hadn't walked by!

Our ideas tumbled over each other. A pile of balloons are in the middle of the room. As quickly as possible everyone tries to pick up a balloon without using hands—which is impossible without someone's help. As soon as two people have "caught a falling star" between them, they can then try to link with others by catching another balloon together until everyone is connected by a balloon star. And when, just for fun, we added that "Catch a Marta Star" could be sung whenever anyone felt victorious, we discovered that the song works as a round. Serendipity!

> *Catch a falling star*
> (or a Marta star or somebody else's name)
> *and put it in your pocket*
> *Save it for a rainy day.*
>
> *Catch a falling star*
> *and put it in your pocket*
> *Never let it fade away.*

—*Mally Cox-Chapman*

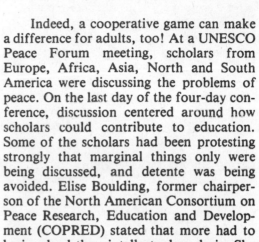

Indeed, a cooperative game can make a difference for adults, too! At a UNESCO Peace Forum meeting, scholars from Europe, Africa, Asia, North and South America were discussing the problems of peace. On the last day of the four-day conference, discussion centered around how scholars could contribute to education. Some of the scholars had been protesting strongly that marginal things only were being discussed, and detente was being avoided. Elise Boulding, former chairperson of the North American Consortium on Peace Research, Education and Development (COPRED) stated that more had to be involved than intellectual analysis. She explained at some length that detente is precarious and difficult and that nothing was going to be solved by people sitting at a table, talking. Since the elements in detente have to do with interdependence, she wanted to illustrate her point metaphorically. She stood up and asked that everyone participate in playing Musical Laps. The scholars responded with varying degrees of puzzlement and enthusiasm. However, all played. It was an excellent experience for the scholars, who got the point of the metaphor. Afterwards, the atmosphere was warmer and more responsive, and people listened more attentively to each other. Musical Laps made a difference!

Changing traditional competitive games

Although traditional competitive games are still deeply rooted in the American school system, there is a growing awareness of their shortcomings which is already beginning to change the very basis of physical education.

I would like to suggest that whenever possible we start changing these old competitive games. Teachers can determinedly persist in introducing games which are cooperative at the same time that they develop skills and improve coordination. Cooperation *is* difficult to teach in physical education programs, mainly because there is such a lack of cooperation in other spheres both in and out of school. However, since it is so important, every small effort in this direction counts. An excellent example of such a small effort is described in Choosing Teams Cooperatively.

There are a variety of reasons for changing some of the competitive elements in traditional team games: 1) if there is limited equipment (such as a badminton set), a rotation system will allow for more than four people to play; 2) if the teacher wants to lessen the effects of competition, a rotation system will retain the accumulation of points and a winning side but the participants will have played on both sides of the net, eliminating their being pitted against one another; 3) if the teacher wants to encourage students to work together cooperatively, the opportunity to create new rules invites more interaction among the students.

Teachers must not be discouraged if the students seem to resist trying some of these activities. To create exciting and challenging new games, teachers and students need to work together. It *is* possible, and it *is* worth the extra effort!

ROUND-ROBIN PING-PONG

Ping-pong is played with two paddles, one at each end of the table. People (at least five or six—preferably nine or ten) are lined up on both sides. Two players with paddles in their hands begin by hitting the ball to one another. As soon as a player has hit the ball, he or she quickly places the paddle on the table and runs to the end of the line. Meanwhile, the next player has picked up the paddle and hits the ball, drops the paddle and quickly moves out of the way of the next person. The ball should be hit gently and slowly until people are confident. (We've been known to hit the ball with our hands when all else fails!)

Participants initially should decide the direction of movement. After a while, people may want to move in the opposite direction. Recently, at a party, we made up a new, wild variation: First, people move in one direction. One of the paddle holders yells, "SWITCH!" which signals everyone to reverse direction. Probably the two paddle holders should hit the ball several times to allow a few extra seconds for participants to switch directions. It's marvelous!

COOPERATIVE BADMINTON

Four participants place themselves on the court, two on a side, and decide how they want to keep score (the regular scoring rules can be used). The remaining participants place themselves along each side of the court, ready to step in. After a point has been made (or two, or three), everyone, both players and standbys, rotates one person to the right (see diagram). People may want to create rules as they go along to make the game easier or more challenging.

COOPERATIVE VOLLEYBALL

This can be played in a fashion similar to badminton. Any number can play or, again, if there are too many, people can wait in line and enter after a point has been made. Another possibility is to see how many times the ball can go over the net before it hits the ground. It has been known to go to one hundred, but even fifty is an exciting number to aim for. To insure maximum participation, perhaps a minimum of three or four people per side should touch/hit the ball before sending it to the other side.

CHOOSING TEAMS COOPERATIVELY
(Pat Cockrell of Friends Central School)

The teacher picks two captains, each of whom picks one team member. Each team member in turn picks someone else, and so on down the line. In this way each team member will get to choose someone, except for the last person picked. Though this method still does not eliminate the "last person picked" embarrassment, usually there is a different last person each time.

Activities for preschoolers

This section is in response to many requests from the people who care about and for preschoolers. Most of the games here are adapted from the cooperative games created for older children. There is no magic. One merely reduces a game to its bare elements, simplifying it so that young children are able to understand and participate fully. Preschool children are creative and open. Their work is learning about their environment through play. They create games all the time. All we adults need to do is to observe them carefully, assuming that they are doing the right thing. If we take cues from their play behavior, we'll know what activities and games are appropriate for them. Because preschoolers learn by repetition, these games will provide endless enjoyment as they are played over and over. Each time an activity is repeated, the child discovers new things about himself or herself, such as competence, cooperation, or a new skill.

The values we are hoping to build are ones of cooperation, caring, fun, a sense of the group, and of respecting, helping, and looking out for each other. Many preschool teachers and day care center staff members are searching for activities which include every member of the group and which encourage participation without the emphasis on competing or winning. It's important for young children to learn that it is possible to play without being pitted against one another. We are interested in providing a supportive atmosphere as well as a time in the day when everyone can be a part of an activity which brings children and adults together in a thoughtful and caring way.

The teacher will naturally sense the tone of the room, whether it is one of restless energy, of angry feelings left over from unresolved conflicts from recess, or even of hot afternoon sleepiness. These short non-competitive activities help to change the atmosphere, break the tension or release the pent-up energy. They are easy, fun, tangible, mainly non-verbal activities which really work. Two skilled Montessori teachers we know sometimes take their class to the gym to play Kangaroo Tag, which allows them to release their bursting energy in an active game. When she sees the children losing attention, a classroom volunteer with whom we worked at the Children's School asks the children to stand, touch toes with each other, wiggle their feet. It's important to begin developing an awareness of their own bodies as everyone plays together. In these activities, no one worries about being first or about not doing well. This allows for the full, rich experience of just being together.

What I would personally wish for the teacher or whoever has the fortunate position of being with young children would be the willingness and flexibility to create these kinds of games on her or his own, either with co-workers or with children themselves. This handbook is only a jumping-off place— an invitation to make up new activities, to stretch the imagination. There is a marvelous sense of satisfaction when an activity is created that everyone enjoys and wants to play again and again. Even as adults, we can recapture that playful spark and fan it alive.

Cooperative games adapted for preschoolers

Because preschool teachers and day care centers have found many of the games listed in the handbook too difficult for their children, some out of necessity have taken the bare essence of a game and have adapted it. Some of these worked and some didn't. Some turned out to be different than one would expect. Karen Zaur's experience of adapting a game may help others to feel more comfortable in trying it, no matter the age.

"One day when I was substitute teaching a class of second and third graders, I decided to teach them Pretzel. They loved getting themselves into a big knot but found it difficult to find a position they would be able to hold while they were untangled. I worried at first that they were doing it wrong because I hadn't explained well enough, but afterwards I realized they had a whole new thing—a knot game!"

To adapt a game for preschoolers, teachers can introduce it in sections, teaching one section at a time until the children become comfortable and familiar with it, then moving on to the next.

Many different elements make a game too con-fusing for most small children and it may need to be adapted. For example, in I'm Going on a Trip, the first four or five children can initiate physical gestures to pass around the circle; then the rest of the children can pass around the same four or five gestures. Doing it is the important thing. After about five gestures, small children forget, get scared, and freeze. So instead of asking for a new gesture, the leader could suggest, "See how many you can remember." If someone wants to add one, fine. If everyone gives the child a big cheer for remembering five of them (with help, if needed), he or she will get better and better at remembering. (See text for full description of this game.)

Touch Blue can be played with any age children. The adult can decide on the kinds of things to be touched. Perhaps children can take turns being the leader.

Pretzel can also be played with the very young, but as Karen Zaur so aptly put it, be prepared for a brand new game!

CATCH A MOUSE

For those times when you need a quiet break, a few moments to catch your breath, say to the children, "Pretend you are going to catch a mouse. You will need to walk very quietly to the rug (to your chairs, etc.) so that you won't scare the little animal." It's challenging for them to see how quiet they can be.

PASS THE MASK

Young children do this well. With the group sitting in a circle, the first person makes a funny face. The second person to the left (or right) makes the same face as the first person, and then makes a face of her or his own. The third person imitates the second person's funny face and also makes one up. Each person in turn makes a mask, and each person imitates the one of the person next in the circle.

A CLOSING CIRCLE is a short activity which draws the children together at the end of a morning or a day, to give a sense of closure. The teacher should choose an activity which reflects something good that happened during the day, or, if the day has been difficult, one which will provide a sense of community or uplift. Two suggestions:

1. **Passing a Hug.** Children stand in a circle. One person starts by giving a hug to the person on the right, and that person in turn gives a hug to the person on his or her right, and so forth around the circle.

2. **Electric Squeeze.** Again people stand in a circle, this time holding hands. One person gently squeezes the hand to his or her left, and that person squeezes the one to his or her left, and so on. The idea is to watch the electric squeeze being passed from person to person, around the circle.

142

RHYTHMIC CLAPPING
(adapted by Sandy Branam)

Here's another game that three, four and five-year-olds seem to love. When they first start, they clap wildly and with not much rhythm, but with practice they get better and better. If you need the attention of the group, you can end the activity by clapping very quietly, which will allow you to speak softly to the class.

KANGAROO HOP (created by two teachers, Sandy Branam and Kathy Young)

This is an energetic tag game used to let out excess energy and it is also a whole lot of fun! If someone gets tagged, he or she is lucky. The lucky person becomes a kangaroo and hops around, trying to tag someone else. As soon as the next person is tagged, that person joins the first person in hopping around and tagging others. In the end, everyone is a lucky hopping kangaroo!

MUSICAL HUGS
(adapted from Switchbacks by Gail Wooten)

Small children seem to enjoy this tremendously. Children walk around the room while music is playing, or the leader is singing. When the music stops, everyone hugs another person. The music starts up again and the whole thing is repeated. The teacher can suggest that they hug a different person each time.

Variation: Try musical backs, musical elbows, etc.

TOUCH NOSE (adapted from Touch Blue by Kathy Allen, day care coordinator)

This is an excellent activity for very young children. They must find a partner and sit or stand close together. Then the adult calls out different parts of the body (e.g., "touch nose") and the children touch each other's noses with their hands or fingers. The adult picks the different parts of the body to be touched.

CORNERS
(adapted by Sandy Branam and Kathy Young)

This game has been used successfully to start young children thinking about choices in solving problems. The choices might begin with, "Which would you rather be—ice cream or cake?" or "blocks or tricycles?" They love moving from one side of the room to the other. Next, the leader could try more thoughtful issues like, "Would you rather be a biter or a slapper?" Since neither is very appealing, they start to think. Having them talk with each other about the reasons for their choices involves them naturally in a discussion about real classroom issues.

DO YOUR EARS HANG LOW?

A song that children want to sing over and over.

"**Do your ears hang low?**" (Make hands into ears.)
"**Do they wobble to and fro?**" (Wiggle fingers back and forth.)
"**Can you tie them in a knot?**" (Hands in front tie a big imaginary knot.)
"**Can you tie them in a bow?**" (Hands in front tie a big imaginary bow.)
"**Can you throw them over your shoulder—**" (Exaggerate throwing them over one shoulder)
"**—like a Continental soldier?**" (Raise right hand, salute style, to forehead.)
"**Do your ears hang low?**" (Put hands by ears again.)

Variation children love: The leader sings along with the children as usual but speeds up or slows down drastically every other phrase, e.g., "Do your ears hang low?" (sung slowly), "Do they wobble to and fro?" (sung quickly). Continue to alternate fast and slow throughout the song.

THREE BLUE PIGEONS

This particular song should be done with a great deal of exaggeration and flair. Children love it!

"**Three blue pigeons, three blue pigeons, three blue pigeons...**"
   (Gesture of three fingers held up, or two fingers, depending on how many pigeons have left or returned. Sing slowly, and show an exaggerated face of sadness or joy, depending on whether the pigeons are leaving or returning.)
"**Sitting on a fence...**"
   (Sing quickly, almost to the point of blurring the words.)
"**Oh, look! One of them has flown a-WAY...**"
   (The right arm is stretched outwards.)
"**What a shame!...**"
   (That same arm is thrown back and bent so one's head can rest in it in sorrow.)
"**Oh, look! One of them has re-turned!...**"
   (Right arm is flung out and flung back towards the body.)
"**Let us re-joice!**"
   (Both hands raised high above the head, waving joyously.)

Verses

2) **two blue pigeons**
3) **one blue pigeon**
4) **no blue pigeons**
5) **one blue pigeon**
6) **two blue pigeons**
7) **three blue pigeons**
end) no spoken part—
unless you want to go on forever!

INDEX OF GAMES

WAYS TO SELF RULE:
BEYOND MARXISM AND ANARCHISM
by George Fischer

How democratic self rule transforms science, school, and community, and how it offers our best alternative to the modern authoritarianism of "1984." Carol Ascher, feminist author: "A lovely book by a much loved professor."

244 pages. Hardbound. $14.95

DESPAIRWORK: AWAKENING TO THE
PERIL AND PROMISE OF OUR TIME
by Joanna Macy

"What we urgently need is to break the taboo against expressions of despair for our world—to validate these feelings of rage and grief, realize their universality, and experience in them the mutual support that can empower us to act. To do despair work is, in a real sense, to wake up—both to the peril and the promise."

32 pages. 1982. $2.45

MOVING TOWARD A NEW SOCIETY
by Susanne Gowan, George Lakey, William Moyer and Richard Taylor.

Move from doomsday ideology to a joyous celebration of struggle. A bold analysis of current social and political conditions, coupled with an exciting vision of a new democratic, decentralized and caring social order, and a nonviolent revolutionary strategy.

"A must for any serious social change activist."
— *Peacework*

296 pages. $5.00

A MODEL FOR NONVIOLENT
COMMUNICATION
by Marshall Rosenberg

This groundbreaking work in interpersonal relations helps us more fully open ourselves to give and receive information, share feelings, and overcome blocks to effective communication. It is filled with illuminating examples.

40 pages. 1983. $3.95

A MANIFESTO FOR NONVIOLENT
REVOLUTION
by George Lakey

Original 1972 working paper analyzing problems of contemporary society, presenting visions of a new society, and a nonviolent strategy for getting there. Excellent for initiating group dialogue.

26 pages. Large format. $1.75

HANDBOOK FOR SATYAGRAHIS:
A MANUAL FOR VOLUNTEERS OF
TOTAL REVOLUTION
by Narayan Desai

India's foremost trainer in nonviolent action presents an integrated, practical approach to training for radical social change, growing out of the experience of the Gandhian movement.

57 pages. $3.95

To Order: send check or money order to New Society Publishers, 4722 Baltimore Avenue, Philadelphia, PA 19143. For postage and handling: add $1.50 for the first book and 40¢ for each additional book.

147

NO BOSSES HERE! A MANUAL ON WORKING COLLECTIVELY AND COOPERATIVELY
by Karen Brandow, Jim McDonnell, and Vocations for Social Change

The title says it all! Down-to-earth, simply written, easy to use. Great for small businesses, co-ops, organizations, church groups.

120 pages. Second edition. $5.95

CLEARNESS: PROCESSES FOR SUPPORTING INDIVIDUALS AND GROUPS IN DECISION-MAKING
by Peter Woodrow

Having trouble making personal decisions? Feeling isolated, alone? Don't know how to utilize other people's good thinking effectively? Handy resource for helping you think about things with the people around, develop trust, tap new resources for support, help people joining new groups. Sample agendas.

32 pages. $2.45

A MANUAL FOR GROUP FACILITATORS
Center for Conflict Resolution

Get your group to work together more effectively. A working manual for learning to communicate well, doing effective planning, solving problems creatively, dealing with conflict, and moving groups toward fulfillment of their own goals.

88 pages. Large format. Illustrated. $6.00

RESOURCE MANUAL FOR A LIVING REVOLUTION
by Virginia Coover, Ellen Deacon, Charles Esser and Christopher Moore

The practical tools you need for everything from consciousness raising, working in groups, and developing communities of support to education, training, and organizing skills. Used by women's groups, disarmament and antinuclear activists, and community organizers worldwide. 25,000 copies in print. An activist's dream!

330 pages. Agendas. Exercises. New edition. 1981. $19.95 (hardbound): $7.95 (paperback)

BUILDING UNITED JUDGEMENT: A HANDBOOK FOR CONSENSUS DECISION MAKING
Center for Conflict Resolution

Reach group unity and make your decision-making structure work for *you*. Maximize cooperation and fully use the creativity of all members of your group. Learn to recognize conflict as a source of growth. Handle common group problems practically.

124 pages. Large format. Illustrated. $6.95

LEADERSHIP FOR CHANGE: TOWARD A FEMINIST MODEL
by Bruce Kokopeli and George Lakey

Reject authoritarian and paternalistic forms of leadership. Making practical use of feminist perspectives, break leadership functions down into their component parts to be shared and rotated, empowering all.

33 pages. Illustrated. $2.45

MEETING FACILITATION: THE NO MAGIC METHOD
by Berit Lakey

Plan and carry out consistently productive meetings. Easy steps to help a group help itself.

11 pages. 50¢

To Order: send check or money order to New Society Publishers, 4722 Baltimore Avenue, Philadelphia PA 19143. For postage and handling: add $1.50 for the first book and 40¢ for each additional book.

THE EYE OF THE CHILD
by Ruth Mueller

A brilliant healing myth for a world gone mad!

"Of all the creatures to whom the great mother had given birth all were a part, not apart, but one. Yes all but one flowed as she flowed, born of her womb, dying in her bosom, struggling, true, but never against their own life support. One, only one, capable of standing apart, imagining self above and outside, turning to rend, turning to overpower, to subdue, to conquer the vessel of life itself, creation's own embodiment. Had she not labored for aeons to give birth to a triumph of joy and beauty as fair as dawn, a creature of light to share the glowing consciousness of the whole, one of understanding as deep as her deeps are deep, of laughter as divine as tears and of tears as cleansing as laughter, one who was no alien to mercy, capable of new visions above predation, a familiar to the art of healing, above all a creature of tongues, creation itself no longer mute to express—to express—

"What had gone wrong?"

Ecological speculative fiction of the highest order.

240 pages. 1984
Paperback: $7.95

WOMEN IN DEVELOPMENT: A RESOURCE GUIDE FOR ORGANIZATION AND ACTION,
by ISIS Women's International Information and Communication Service.

A lavishly illustrated book, with 122 photographs, five years in the making. Women scholars from all over the world contributed to make this one of the most comprehensive and beautiful books of its kind ever published. Sections on women and multinationals, women and rural development, women and health, education, tourism, migration, etc.

Annotated resource lists, bibliographies. 240 pages. 1984.
Hardcover: $39.95
Paperback: $14.95

NO TURNING BACK: LESBIAN AND GAY LIBERATION FOR THE '80s
by Gerre Goodman, George Lakey, Judy Lashof and Erika Thorne; Foreword by Malcolm Boyd

"*No Turning Back* fulfills a long felt need for a progressive analysis and pragmatic sourcebook for lesbians, gays and others concerned with replacing patriarchal oppression with a more human alternative. I was quite pleased by the integration of personal statements and experiences into the more theoretical discussion, and by the inclusion of practical and feasible proposals for individual and collective action."

> —Larry Gross, Professor, Annenberg School of Communications, University of Pennsylvania, and Co-Chair, Philadelphia Lesbian and Gay Task Force

Recommended for public libraries by *Library Journal*.

168 pages.
Hardcover: $16.95
Paperback: $7.95

TWO ESSAYS: ON ANGER and NEW MEN, NEW WOMEN Some Thoughts on Nonviolence
by Barbara Deming

Thought-provoking essays adding new depth to the slogan that 'the personal is political'. Modern classics in the literature of nonviolent struggle, challenging us to recreate ourselves even as we attempt to recreate our world. Originally appeared in Barbara Deming's *We Can Not Live Without Our Lives*.

32 pages. 1982. $2.45

OFF THEIR BACKS...AND ON OUR OWN TWO FEET
by Men Against Patriarchy

This pamphlet addressed to men includes three essays: "More Power Than We Want: Masculine Sexuality and Violence," "Understanding and Fighting Sexism," and "Overcoming Masculine Oppression in Mixed Groups."

32 pages. 1983. $2.45

To Order: send check or money order to New Society Publishers, 4722 Baltimore Avenue, Philadelphia PA 19143. For postage and handling: add $1.50 for the first book and 40¢ for each additional book.

149

GANDHI THROUGH WESTERN EYES
by Horace Alexander

"This book stands out as an authoritative guide: clear, simple, and straightforward, both to Gandhi's personality and to his beliefs. As a Quaker, Mr. Alexander found it easy to grasp Gandhi's ideas about non-violence; the author's prolonged and intimate friendship helped him to know the Mahatma as few men were able to do, and to appreciate that he was something far greater than a national hero of the Indian independence movement—a man, in fact, with a message that is intensely relevant for the world today. Nothing that has so far been published about Gandhi is more illuminating than this careful, perceptive and comprehensive work. It is not only comprehensive—it is convincing."   —Times Literary Supplement

Letter, Index, 240 pages. 1984
Hardcover: $24.95
Paperback: $8.95

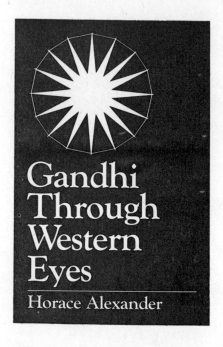

MORE THAN THE TROUBLES: A COMMON SENSE VIEW OF THE NORTHERN IRELAND CONFLICT
by Lynne Shivers and David Bowman, S.J.; foreword by Denis Barritt; afterword by Joseph Fahey, S.J. on "Northern Ireland: Its Relevance for Peace Education".

"No stereotypes about Northern Ireland and its people, its religion, or politics can survive a reading of this carefully constructed account of a packed and eventful history where past and future compete for attention in the present. The juxtaposition of bitter conflict and cooperation makes this story a microcosm of the human condition in this century. The difficult task of documentation is done with loving care. As readers we are at once humbled, sobered, and inspired . . . . "
          —Dr. Elise Boulding, Professor of Sociology, Dartmouth College and the University of Colorado; founder of COPRED (Consortium on Peace Research, Education and Development)

Index, appendices, maps, charts, bibliography, photographs. 240 pages. 1984. Hardcover: $24.95

To Order: send check or money order to New Society Publishers, 4722 Baltimore Avenue, Philadelphia, PA 19143. For postage and handling: add $1.50 for the first book and 40¢ for each additional book.

WE ARE ALL PART OF ONE ANOTHER: A BARBARA DEMING READER

"I have had the dream that women should at last be the ones to truly experiment with nonviolent struggle, discover its full force."

Essays, speeches, letters, stories, poems by America's foremost writer on issues of women and peace, feminism and nonviolence, spanning four decades. Lovingly edited by activist-writer Jane Meyerding; Black feminist writer Barbara Smith, founder of Kitchen Table Press, has graciously contributed a foreword. A book no activist of the '80s will want to be without.

"Barbara Deming is the voice of conscience for her generation and all those to follow, measured in reason, compassionate, clear, requiring: the voice of a friend."
—Jane Rule

"Wisdom, modesty, responsiveness, love: all of these qualities live in her writings, a treasured gift to the world."
—Leah Fritz

320 pages. 1984
Hardcover: $24.95
Paperback: $10.95

REWEAVING THE WEB OF LIFE: FEMINISM AND NONVIOLENCE
edited by Pam McAllister

". . . happens to be one of the most important books you'll ever read."
—*The Village Voice*

"Stressing the connection between patriarchy and war, sex and violence, this book makes it clear that nonviolence can be an assertive, positive force. It's provocative reading for anyone interested in surviving and changing the nuclear age."
—*Ms. Magazine*

More than 50 Contributors–Women's History–Women and the Struggle Against Militarism–Violence and Its Origins–Nonviolence and Women's Self-Defense–Interviews –Songs–Poems–Stories–Provocative Proposals–Photographs–Annotated Bibliography–Index

Voted "Best New Book—1983—*WIN MAGAZINE ANNUAL BOOK POLL*

448 pages.
Hardcover: $19.95
Paperback: $10.95

To Order: send check or money order to New Society Publishers, 4722 Baltimore Avenue, Philadelphia, PA 19143. For postage and handling: add $1.50 for the first book and 40¢ for each additional book.

"This is the bravest book I have read since Jonathan Schell's FATE OF THE EARTH." —Dr. Rollo May

DESPAIR AND PERSONAL POWER IN THE NUCLEAR AGE
by Joanna Rogers Macy

Despair and Personal Power in the Nuclear Age is the first major book to examine our psychological responses to planetary perils and to lay the theoretical foundations for an empowering, personally-centered approach to social change. Included are sections on awakening in the nuclear age, relating to children and young people, guided meditations, empowerment rituals, and a special section on "Spiritual Exercises for a Time of Apocalypse." As described and excerpted in *New Age Journal* and *Fellowship Magazine*. Recommended for public libraries by *Library Journal;* selected for inclusion in the 1984 Women's Reading Program, General Board of Global Ministries, United Methodist Church.

200 pages. Appendices, resource lists, exercises. 1983.
Hardcover: $19.95
Paperback: $8.95

RAINBOWS NOT RADIATION!
BANANAS NOT BOMBS!
GRAPES NOT GUNS!
XYLOPHONES NOT X-TINCTION!

WATERMELONS NOT WAR! A SUPPORT BOOK FOR PARENTING IN THE NUCLEAR AGE
by Kate Cloud, Ellie Deegan, Alice Evans, Hayat Imam, and Barbara Signer; Afterword by Dr. Helen Caldicott

Five mothers in the Boston area have been meeting regularly for four years, to give each other support, to demystify nuclear technology—weapons and technology—into terms parents, *and children,* can understand, to find ways of acting which will give their children a future. The result is WATERMELONS NOT WAR! A SUPPORT BOOK FOR PARENTING IN THE NUCLEAR AGE.

—As written up in *Ms. Magazine, Whole Life Times, Sojourner.*

Large format. Beautifully illustrated.
Annotated Bibliography. 160 pages. 1984.
Hardcover: $24.95
Paperback: $9.95

To Order: send check or money order to New Society Publishers, 4722 Baltimore Avenue, Philadelphia, PA 19143. For postage and handling: add $1.50 for the first book and 40¢ for each additional book.